MW00608131

FREEDOM
CLASS MANUAL

Freedom Class Manual

Knowing Christ Intimately. Experiencing Life Abundantly.
by Brian Brennt and Mike Riches
Fourth Edition, May 2010
Copyright © 2007 by Brian Brennt and Mike Riches

All rights reserved. No part of this publication may be reproduced, stored in a retrieval system, or transmitted in any form by any means, electronic, mechanical, photocopy, recording or otherwise, without the prior permission of the publisher, except as provided by USA copyright law.

Scripture quotations marked (ESV) are from The Holy Bible, English Standard Version, copyright © 2001 by Crossway Bibles, a division of Good News Publishers. Used by permission. All rights reserved.

Scriptures marked (NASB) are from the New American Standard Bible ®, Copyright © 1960, 1962, 1963, 1968, 1971, 1972, 1973, 1975, 1977, 1995 by The Lockman Foundation. Used by permission. www.lockman.org.

Scriptures marked (NKJV) are from The New King James Version ®. Copyright © 1982 by Thomas Nelson Inc. Used by permission. All rights reserved.

Scriptures marked (NLT) are taken from the Holy Bible, New Living Translation, copyright © 1996. Used by permission of Tyndale House Publishers, Inc., Wheaton, Illinois 60189.

Scriptures marked (NIV) are taken from the Holy Bible, NEW INTERNATIONAL VERSION ®. Copyright © 1973, 1978, 1984 International Bible Society. All rights reserved throughout the world. Used by permission of International Bible Society.

Scriptures marked (MSG) have been taken from The Message ®. Copyright © 1993, 1994, 1995, 1996, 2000, 2001, 2002. Used by permission of NavPress Publishing Group.

Any bold or underlining within the text has been added for emphasis.

Published by: City Central Publishing
                2522 N. Proctor St, #1,
                Tacoma, Washington 98406
                www.citycentral.org

To Contact: Phone: 253-404-0177
                Email: info@citycentral.org

Printed in South Korea
ISBN 978-1-934290-00-2
Cover and Book Design: Pete Mahoney, Josh Read
Editing: Pete Mahoney
Proofing: Nicholas Gorne, Alexis Phillips, Harry & Hen Ferdinando

---

TABLE OF CONTENTS

Introduction: What is Freedom? 01

[1] **The Power of Salvation** 05

[2] **Our Original Design** 11

[3] **Strongholds** 17

[4] **The Authority of the Believer** 25

[5] **Effects of Injustice** 31

[6] **Blessings and Curses** 37

[7] **Intercession & Breaking
     Generational Patterns** 43

STRONGHOLD WORKSHEETS

Anger 53
Fear 60
Passivity 63
Rejection 67
Shame 74
Unforgiveness 79

READING HOMEWORK

Study on Spiritual Warfare 86
What is Repentance? 91
Breaking Free, Part 1 93
Breakthrough in Discipline 96
Our World Has Two Realms 99

RESOURCE SECTION

The Christian's Birthright 104
God's Love and Forgiveness 106
Walking in the Opposite Spirit 108

WHAT IS FREEDOM?

WHAT IS THE FREEDOM CLASS ALL ABOUT?

God has an incredible purpose for us in this life. We get to know and love the God of the universe, and even participate in His plans! Our amazing privilege is to live for the *glory of God*, that His name and His fame would be spread throughout the earth. And if this were not enough, Jesus has promised us abundant life and joy not dependent on any life circumstance.

John 10:10 (NASB) *The thief comes only to steal and kill and destroy; I came that they may have life, and have it abundantly.*

Even though we know all the promises of Scripture are true, it easy to lose focus and become weighed down with cares, defeat, past hurts, hopelessness, and other areas of sin that keep us in bondage. These hindrances steal our intimacy with Christ and the joy of our salvation. Freedom is about being released to love and serve Jesus wholeheartedly.

Put simply, the Freedom Class is about becoming more like Jesus and reflecting His love and power to everyone around us. Freedom is not just about changing behavior, but about letting God change our <u>very being</u>. The goal of the class is not to learn new information that we can store on a dusty bookshelf. The goal is transformation, and the time is now!

THE FOUNDATION: THE CROSS OF CHRIST

The essence of salvation is freedom. Freedom is not a separate component of the gospel; rather, it is the very heart of the gospel message. **Freedom is what Christ brought us through His death and resurrection.** Take a look at what Christ has done for all of us:

2 Corinthians 1:10 (NKJV) [It is God] *who delivered us from so great a death, and does deliver us, in whom we trust that He will still deliver us.*

1. We are delivered from the penalty of sin: shame, guilt, condemnation, and death.

2. We are set free from the power of sin. Because of the power of Christ, we are no longer controlled by the power of sin. Before Christ came into our hearts we were slaves to sin. And as slaves, we were powerless to gain victory over our oppressor or our flesh and sin nature. However, because of Jesus, we now have power to say no to sin and all of its temptations (see Romans 6-8).

3. It is important to understand that when Jesus returns we will be delivered from the very presence of sin and all of its destruction. But before that day, we are in a battle.

+definition+
- FREEDOM -

Discovering your identity and purpose in Jesus and tearing down every stronghold that opposes your ability to walk in the fullness of that identity and purpose.

WHAT MUST BE UNDERSTOOD TO LIVE IN FREEDOM?

1. The meaning and fullness of **salvation**.

2. The **calling** and **destiny** Christ has for you.

3. **How to tear down strongholds**.

4. The effects of an absence of **love and truth** in your life.

5. How sin gives the enemy **jurisdiction** (a place of power) in your life.

6. The power and simplicity of genuine **repentance**.

7. Understanding the **power** that is yours in Christ at salvation.

8. How to **take back territory** from the enemy in your life and home.

Expanding this definition will help you to gain a fuller understanding of the exciting truths you will learn and experience in this class.

FREEDOM: AN EXPANDED DEFINITION

1. **Jesus has a specific purpose for your life**. The kingdom of God is not random and neither is your life. Jesus came to give you abundant life, so that you might reflect His glory. He has lavished you with His love! To really accept and move in your purpose as a child of God, you must accept the love and favor of Christ. As you live in His love, you will gain the confidence needed to fight against any strongholds that hold you back from moving in your purpose (2 Corinthians 10:3-5, John 10:10).

2. **Jesus never loses and always leads us in overwhelming victory.** Loss is not in His game plan. Through His power, you are more than a conqueror! You have the ability to rip off every hindrance and chain in which you have been bound by the enemy (Romans 8:37).

3. **The very word "freedom" implies war.** Only the broken, the desperate, and the weak are equipped to win this war. The weapons that are yours in Christ are so powerful that nothing in hell can withstand them. Freedom comes when you stand firmly behind our commander, Jesus Christ, in full allegiance to Him. The more you radically obey all that He asks of you, the faster strongholds are demolished and joy is released in your life (John 8:31-32, Ephesians 6:12).

4. **Realize that Satan is a thief and a destroyer.** He desires your destruction, and he desperately wants to steal all good things from your life. Freedom is about the realization that only through taking your sins to the cross and receiving God's forgiveness will you win this battle. The deeper your repentance, the more territory you take back in your life (John 10:10, 1 John 1:9).

WHAT IS THE PURPOSE OF DISMANTLING STRONGHOLDS?

We are created to have an intimate relationship with Jesus! The primary purpose for dismantling strongholds is so that we can experience His love in a deeper way. In the Freedom Class, we do go after sin patterns and strongholds. The main reason for this is to remove any obstacles that separate us from God. Imagine life as a pipe: If the pipe is clogged with debris (strongholds), then the water (God's love and power) is unable to flow through effectively. When we unclog a pipe, we do not keep the debris as a prize. In the same way, the goal of pursuing freedom is not to focus on our strongholds, but to focus on removing them for the purpose of experiencing God's love in a more intimate way. Our prize is a greater revelation of Christ!

Here is a more thorough answer to the question, "What is the purpose of dismantling strongholds?"

1. **To know and understand the character and nature of God.**

   Romans 12:2 (NLT) *Don't copy the behavior and customs of this world, but let God transform you into a new person by changing the way you think. Then you will know what God wants you to do, and you will know how good and pleasing and perfect his will really is.*

   Strongholds are composed of thoughts, attitudes, and beliefs that do not reflect the character of God. As we dismantle strongholds in our lives, we can more clearly know and understand the true character and nature of God. Consider the following examples:

   Stronghold of passivity:
   There is never passivity in Jesus' love for each one of us! God never hesitates in His forgiveness or approval. God does not forget what He has promised, nor does He need to be reminded to be outward focused. God moves in initiation toward each of us. "You see, at just the right time, when we were still powerless, Christ died for the ungodly" (Romans 5:6, NIV). As we read about Jesus in the Gospels, there is no passivity in the demonstration of His love, mercy, and compassion toward those around Him. This realization helps us understand why passivity falls so short of the character of God. As we realize that the character of God's love is selfless, initiatory, and bold, we grow in intimacy with Christ. Jesus did not respond to the Father in passivity on the way to the cross! His actions force us to re-evaluate our own level of obedience.

   Stronghold of unforgiveness:
   God never withholds forgiveness for those who come to Him. We are completely forgiven for our sins through the work of Jesus on the cross! God does not function in resentment toward us or carry a personal grudge over our sin. He does not sit around complaining and criticizing us behind our backs. God is patient and enduring in His love toward us—we cannot wear God out! God never thinks about whether or not He is going to forgive us, nor does He say, "I forgive you," but not mean it. God rejoices over just one sinner who repents (Luke 15). He does not compare us to other people, nor pout when we refuse to do what He asks. His nature and character is love, and it is unconditional. As we remove bitterness, resentment, and buried anger from our lives (by granting full forgiveness to people), we will begin to walk in a greater revelation of the love Christ has for us. We will become more and more like Christ, and therefore have deeper intimacy and joy in our relationship with God as well.

2. Freedom drives us to understand God's love more deeply.

Romans 8:38-39 (NIV) *For I am convinced that neither death nor life, neither angels nor demons, neither the present nor the future, nor any powers, neither height nor depth, nor anything else in all creation, will be able to separate us from the love of God that is in Christ Jesus our Lord.*

God wants us to know the height, depth, and length of the love of Christ. He wants us to have personal revelation of this love so that we can live confidently in it. As we grow in understanding of Jesus' love for us and receive it in our hearts deeply—transformation follows. The Lord wants to open up our hearts and minds to a revelation of His immense love for us. Then we can come closer to loving like he does. Everything a Christian does should be done in love (1 Corinthians 16:14).

Examine the following verses regarding the love of Christ:

- Christians have no excuse for not loving "because the love of God has been poured out within our hearts through the Holy Spirit who was given to us" (Romans 5:5).

- We are therefore told to "pursue love" (1 Corinthians 14:1).

- To "put on love" (Colossians 3:14).

- To "increase and abound in love" (1 Thessalonians 3:12; Philippians 1:9).

- To be "sincere in love" (2 Corinthians 8:8).

- To be "unified in love" (Philippians 2:2).

- To be "fervent in love" (1 Peter 4:8).

- To "encourage one another to love" (Hebrews 10:24).

Freedom drives us deeper into the transformational knowledge of Christ. Strongholds stand in the way of our ability to love others as Christ loves us. The freedom of Christ renews our minds and the way we think.

Examples to consider:

Stronghold of fear:
Fear restricts us from truly expressing the passions of our hearts. Fear of other people keeps us living in other people's minds—constantly seeking their approval. Fear constricts us from stepping into our true design and destiny. The Bible tells us that, *"There is no fear in love. But perfect love drives out fear, because fear has*

to do with punishment. The one who fears is not made perfect in love" (1 John 4:18, NIV). The stronghold of fear keeps us at a distance so that we never truly experience the depth of Jesus' love for us. As more and more fear is removed, greater trust and peace will pour out of our lives.

Stronghold of unbelief:
Unbelief is deadly to our hearts and minds because it hinders God's presence and power in our lives. In addition, unbelief makes us critical, leads us to independence (pride and arrogance), and discourages others. Matthew 13:58 (NLT) says, "And so he did only a few miracles there because of their unbelief." On the contrary, Matthew 21:22 (NLT) says, "If you believe, you will receive whatever you ask for in prayer." If we do not see many miracles around us, it is possible that we are riddled with unbelief. Unbelief never allows for God to lavish us with his love and provision. He wants to pour out on us in every way possible. He is so generous! But unbelief can hinder us from simply accepting his love, forgiveness, and outpouring.

FREEDOM IS ABOUT A DEEP AND POWERFULLY INTIMATE RELATIONSHIP WITH JESUS CHRIST!

GROUND RULES FOR THIS CLASS

1. You will be given your instructor's email address to contact him or her with any questions that might surface.

2. Bring a Bible to the class. You always want to be saturated in the Word of God!

3. Make a commitment to attend every class and complete the homework given to you. Each class builds on the last, and it is detrimental to miss class.

4. Remember that you are invading territory that the enemy has held for many years in some cases. Regular church attendance is imperative as you tear down strongholds. You want to be filled with worship and truth as you fight! You cannot tackle this alone! You need your brothers and sisters in Christ to aid you as you move forward in freedom.

5. Bible reading is crucial. There are also some weekly reading assignments for homework. All the readings are at the back of the book. Take the time to read through these assignments as they offer additional learning that will give you a well-rounded view of the topics discussed in class.

THE POWER OF SALVATION

WHAT DOES IT MEAN TO BE SAVED?

Luke 19:10 (NIV) *For the Son of Man came to seek and to save what was lost.*

What does it mean to actually be saved? How does Scripture describe salvation? Why is it so important to understand?

The Greek word for save in Luke 19:10 is *sozo.* This word communicates the full meaning of salvation.

Sozo encompasses many different aspects of salvation:

1. Deliverance.
2. Restoration.
3. Protection.
4. Preservation.
5. Healing.
6. Making whole.

Look at the six words above. They are a great description of what Jesus had in mind when He ministered. Does this definition of salvation change your perspective? Had you limited salvation to eternal life? Sozo gives us a much fuller understanding of the richness of our salvation.

It is exciting to know what it means to be saved! Can you begin to imagine all he has planned for you? The love of Christ is so deep!

WHAT DOES THE WORD "LOST" REALLY MEAN?

Ephesians 1:7 (NLT) *He is so rich in kindness that He purchased our freedom through the blood of His Son, and our sins are forgiven.*

John 8:34 (NIV) *Jesus replied, "I tell you the truth, everyone who sins is a slave to sin."*

Without a relationship with Jesus Christ we are truly lost, but what does "lost" really mean? Why are we lost without Jesus? What have we lost that only a relationship with Jesus Christ can restore?

The common definition for "lost" (found in *Webster's Dictionary*) provides real insight about what it means to be lost. Look at the definition below and consider what it means practically.

1. **Lost: *not made use of, not won or claimed.*** Salvation restores our purpose, which, prior to salvation, we had not "used" or "claimed." However, we can be saved for many years and still not make use of our purpose. Instead, we continue to function in the purpose *we* have chosen for ourselves. In this scenario, Jesus is given only a small piece of our life to use for His purposes. Typically, crisis or hardship will drive us to consider the Lord's plan, but once the crisis has passed we return to our own purposes.

2. **Lost: *no longer possessed or no longer known.*** Prior to salvation, our design was lost. Christ's plan for our life was not known. His love for us was not known. Eternal life was not possessed. Jesus' love for those around us was not known. Forgiveness for our sins was not known.

3. **Lost: *ruined or destroyed physically or morally.*** Our mind was ruined and completely consumed with self. Salvation restores our mind and transforms our heart (Romans 12:1-2).

4. **Lost: *taken away or beyond reach or attainment.*** Our fulfillment and significance was diminished because of our sin. We are unable, through our own actions, to be made right with God. Because of this deficit of fulfillment, all men and women are in a constant search for significance. We go from activity to activity, relationship to relationship, purchase to purchase, but remain empty after these pursuits. Our significance only comes through a restored relationship with God in Jesus Christ, and a revelation of our design and purpose.

WHY DO WE NEED TO BE SAVED?

Why do we need to be concerned with the concept of being saved, or salvation? What does deliverance, restoration, healing, making whole, etc. mean? What am I being saved from?

IN THE BEGINNING

Humankind was created to live in perfect relationship with God, in a beautiful garden with a perfect environment. There was no sin, crime, heartache, sorrow, disease, or death. Adam and Eve had a literal walking and talking relationship with God. But the Scriptures make it clear that these two sinned, they disobeyed God, and could no longer have this same special relationship.

Immediately after Adam and Eve sinned, all humankind was separated from God. Death entered into the world. It was not long before the world was filled with jealousy, anger, hatred, abuse, murder and every other sin.
Scripture states that every person born since has sinned.

Romans 3:23 (NASB) . . . *for all have sinned and fall short of the glory of God. . .*

WHAT IS SIN?

Sin is a violation of God's nature and character—His glory. He is infinite and perfect in love, mercy, righteousness, justice, truth, and goodness (just to name a few). When we fail to love, be merciful, righteous, act justly, or tell the truth (just to name a few), we sin. Sin is not merely the physical act of doing wrong, but a wrong heart toward God. God's standard is a righteousness of heart.

THE CONSEQUENCE?

The Bible states very clearly that all who sin will suffer death and punishment. This death is not merely physical; it is a ruining of relationships, health, and eternal separation from God and the glorious existence of His heaven.

Romans 6:23 (NLT) *For the wages of sin is death, but the free gift of God is eternal life through Christ Jesus our Lord.*

This punishment is not only temporal, with all that is lost on this earth from not operating in God's original design for us and our world, but it is eternal, everlasting. Because God is *just,* He must punish sin. Scripture is clear that there is an eternal punishment of separation from God due to our sin, and there is only one way to resolve this situation.

HOW CAN I BE SAVED?

RECOGNIZE YOUR NEED
The road to restoration and salvation begins with admitting our need. This is difficult for most of us because humility is required to admit that we have violated God, that we are sinners in desperate need of God. Such humility is central to our entire Christian life and path of restoration.

There is a question we can ask ourselves that will help us recognize our need: **"What must I do to be as righteous (holy, perfect) as God is righteous?"** There are not enough good works that we can do to erase our sin and make us as righteous as God! **We must humbly admit we are sinners in need of God's grace. . .**

REALIZE THE SOLUTION
JESUS! Jesus is the only solution. He was fully God, yet He was fully a man. He lived a sinless life on earth. Being God, He actually lived out the righteousness of God. He then died on the cross, was buried for three days and resurrected from the dead. Through the resurrection, He conquered sin and the judgment of sin, which is death. He suffered the punishment of our sin for us.

2 Corinthians 5:21 (NASB) *He made Him who knew no sin to be sin on our behalf, so that we might become the righteousness of God in Him.*

Hebrews 2:14-15 (NLT) *Because God's children are human beings—made of flesh and blood—Jesus also became flesh and blood by being born in human form. For only as a human being could he die, and only by dying could he break the power of the Devil, who had the power of death. Only in this way could he deliver those who have lived all their lives as slaves to the fear of dying.*

John 14:6 (NLT) *Jesus told him, "I am the way, the truth, and the life. No one can come to the Father except through me."*

APPLY THE SOLUTION
It is impossible for us to earn God's righteousness—it is out of our reach. We must receive it as a gift. That is exactly what God has arranged for us.

- You must agree with God in regards to your need for His righteousness because of your sin.
- You must believe that Jesus Christ is fully God who became fully man, but without sin.
- You must believe that He died on the cross to pay for the punishment of your sin and resurrected from death, conquering the power of sin.
- Then you must pray in faith, declaring you believe the truths just stated. Receive God's forgiveness for your sin, and declare you want to become a child of God and that, with God's help, you will devote your life to following Him.

You cannot earn this amazing gift! You do not deserve this wonderful gift. God's plan is that you freely receive His gift of eternal life and salvation by His grace through faith. You cannot do enough good things to earn God's righteousness. You cannot be religious enough to receive God's righteousness. He simply gives it to you as a gift of absolute grace.

God then declares that you are fully righteous even though you have sinned. The Bible uses the legal term *justification* to explain this truth. Even though you are guilty of sin, through Jesus Christ, God declares you innocent; you are righteous with His righteousness. Jesus made an exchange and took your sin and gave you His righteousness!

Titus 3:3-5 (NLT) *Once we, too, were foolish and disobedient. We were misled by others and became slaves to many wicked desires and evil pleasures. Our lives were full of evil and envy. We hated others, and they hated us. But then God our Savior showed us his kindness and love. He saved us, not because of the good things we did, but because of his mercy. He washed away our sins and gave us a new life through the Holy Spirit.*

Romans 10:9-10 (NLT) *For if you confess with your mouth that Jesus is Lord and believe in your heart that God raised him from the dead, you will be saved. For it is by believing in your heart that you are made right with God, and it is by confessing with your mouth that you are saved.*

Romans 10:13 (NLT) *Anyone who calls on the name of the Lord will be saved.*

Ephesians 2:8-9 (NLT) *God saved you by his special favor when you believed. And you can't take credit for this; it is a gift from God. Salvation is not a reward for the good things we have done, so none of us can boast about it.*

UNDERSTANDING REPENTANCE
What was just described is more than mere words or a belief system. It is an action that involves every fiber of your being. It saturates your entire life. It includes your mind, will, emotions, and physical body. Truly being saved is an act of repentance.

HOW DOES REPENTANCE FIT INTO SALVATION?

Faith and repentance are never mutually exclusive. One cannot have faith in Jesus Christ and ignore living in repentance. Theologian Wayne Grudem defines repentance as:

"a heartfelt sorrow for sin, a renouncing of it, and a sincere commitment to forsake it and walk in obedience to Christ." [1] True repentance will result in a changed life. According to Scripture, the fruit of repentance is a changed life. A truly repentant person immediately begins to walk away from old patterns. Repentance is something that occurs in the heart and involves the whole person in a decision to turn from sin.

It is important to realize that mere sorrow for your actions, or even deep remorse over your actions, does not represent genuine repentance. Genuine repentance must be accompanied by a sincere decision to turn your back on sin. Paul wrote:

Acts 20:21 (NIV) *I have declared to both Jews and Greeks that they must turn to God in repentance and have faith in our Lord Jesus.*

He wrote that he rejoiced over the Corinthians not simply because they were grieved, but because they were grieved to the point of repenting.

2 Corinthians 7:9-10 (NASB) *For the sorrow that is according to the will of God produces a repentance without regret, leading to salvation, but the sorrow of the world produces death.*

A worldly sort of grief may involve great sorrow and guilt for one's actions and probably also a fear of punishment, but no genuine renouncing of sin or a commitment to forsake it in one's life.

In Hebrews 12:17 Esau wept over the consequences of his actions, but did not truly repent.

The prior Scriptures make the case that repentance and faith are two sides of the coin of salvation and cannot be separated. It is not that a person first turns from sin and then trusts in Christ or first trusts in Christ and then turns from sin. They occur at the same time.

When we turn to Christ for salvation from our sins, we are at the same time turning away from the sin. If that were not true, turning to Christ for salvation from sin could hardly be considered genuine repentance.

Therefore, it is clearly contrary to the New Testament evidence to speak about having true saving faith without any repentance for sin. It is also contrary to the New Testament to speak about the possibility of someone accepting Christ as their Savior but not as their Lord if that means simply depending on Him for salvation but not committing oneself to forsake sin and to be obedient to Christ from that point forward. [2]

WHAT DOES IT MEAN TO MAKE A COMMITMENT TO JESUS?

To clarify what it means to make a commitment to Jesus as our Savior and Lord let us consider the word "conversion."

It means turning and represents a complete spiritual turn; a turning from sin to Christ. To be saved is more than just head knowledge. It is more than knowing a set of facts about salvation and agreeing with a list of creeds. In order to have a relationship with God, we must have complete dependence on Jesus for salvation. *He* must save us.

Saving faith is personal trust in Jesus Christ for the forgiveness of my sins and for eternal life with God.

The word trust is critical because it implies a personal commitment between *you* and *Jesus*. Just like any relationship, without trust there is neither real friendship nor intimacy. You are putting your trust in Jesus for forgiveness of sin. At salvation the life of trust is birthed and continues to grow as you obey the Lord.

John 1:12 (NIV) *To all who received him, who believed in his name, he gave power to become children of God.*

John 3:16 (NIV) *. . . whoever believes in him should not perish but have eternal life.*

Salvation is about having a personal relationship with Jesus Christ. It is an *act of the will* and a conscious decision. By accepting Christ, you willfully accept the gift of God through Jesus Christ to be saved from the penalty of sin.

SALVATION IS COMPLETED YET ONGOING

We have just learned that salvation is a completely finished work in the person of Jesus Christ. Yet it is ongoing!

Hebrews 10:14 (NIV) *For by that one offering he <u>perfected forever</u> all those whom he is <u>making holy</u>.*

1. **Understanding the promises of salvation.**

   Salvation [as described in Scripture] promises deliverance from the penalty and power of sin. After salvation, we are clean before God. God sees us as our restored self TODAY!

   2 Corinthians 5:17 (NIV) *Therefore, if anyone is in Christ, he is a new creation; the old has gone, the new has come!*

2. **Positionally, salvation is a finished work; practically, it is an ongoing work.**

   The fullness of Jesus Christ is deposited in us at salvation. We live with His person, His character, and His image being released in our life in increasing measures of righteousness, holiness, love, etc.

   Philippians 2:12 (NIV) *Therefore, my dear friends, as you have always obeyed—not only in my presence, but now much more in my absence—continue to work out your salvation with fear and trembling.*

SALVATION IS ABOUT COMPLETE LIFE RESTORATION

Remember *sozo?* Each word in the scriptures below that are bold is a translation of the greek word *sozo*.

1. **Restoration of our relationship with God.**

   Romans 10:9 (NIV) *If you confess with your mouth, "Jesus is Lord," and believe in your heart that God raised him from the dead, you will be **saved**.*

   We are reunited with our Creator and given the chance to live with Him again in eternity. We are forgiven for our sin and are made whole in Jesus Christ.

2. **Restoration of our purpose.**

   2 Timothy 1:9 (NIV) *who has **saved** us and called us to a holy life—not because of anything we have done but because of his own purpose and grace.*

   We are also given a restored purpose and begin to see that He has called each one of us to a great and mighty assignment. Just like Adam, God created each of us with purpose. By His power and restoration we are given the chance to join Him again in His plan, on His path.

3. **Restoration of our inner person.**

   Luke 8:36 (NIV) *And those who had seen it reported to them how the man who was demon-possessed had been **made well**.*

   Jesus releases those that are held captive by the powers of the enemy. No power of the enemy can stand against the power of Christ!

   Luke 7:50 (NASB) *And He said to the woman, "Your Faith has **saved** you; go in peace."*

   Jesus restores our whole life. By His power, we are able to escape the personal bondage caused by sin. He frees us from our past experiences and hurts and leads us in a life of freedom!

4. **Restoration of our physical body.**

   Mark 10:52 (NIV) *And Jesus said to him, "Go your way; your faith has **made you well**." And immediately he regained his sight and began following Him on the road.*

   Jesus can remove any obstacle, including physical ailments. He created us, and He suffers with us when our bodies are not whole. He has sovereign purposes (that we will never understand) about why He releases or withholds physical healing. But Christ's heart is for all to be healed!

(ENDNOTES)

1.   Wayne Grudem, *Systematic Theology (Grand Rapids: Zondervan, 1994),* p. 713

2.   The section "How does Repentance Fit into Salvation?" is an adaptation of "Faith and Repentance Must Come Together," Wayne Grudem, *Systematic Theology (Grand Rapids: Zondervan, 1994),* p. 713-714. *This is a highly recommended resource!*

APPLICATION

Closing Questions

You now have the opportunity to make an informed decision about making a personal commitment to Jesus Christ.

1. Have you personally put your trust in Jesus Christ for your salvation?

You now have the opportunity to recommit your life to Jesus Christ.

2. Is it time to put your full trust back into Jesus? Are you ready to return to your first love?

Write down some thoughts on what you have learned . . .

3. How has your understanding of salvation grown from this teaching?

Group Prayer Declaration

Jesus can restore my purpose! Jesus can restore my marriage! Jesus can heal my mind!
Jesus came to restore, deliver, heal, protect!
Jesus can make me whole, He can set me free!

Homework

In preparation for the next class, read the first homework assignment at the back of the book titled *Study on Spiritual Warfare* [pg. 86]. The battle in this class is not just in our minds and hearts, but also in the spiritual realm. Take the time to go over these scriptures in order to prepare your heart for this battle.

NOTES:

OUR ORIGINAL DESIGN

GOD'S MASTERPIECE

Ephesians 2:10 (NLT) *For we are God's masterpiece. He has created us anew in Christ Jesus, so that we can do the good things he planned for us long ago.*

Acts 17:26 (NIV) *From one man he made every nation of men, that they should inhabit the whole earth; and he determined the times set for them and the exact places where they should live.*

Psalm 139:13 (NASB) *For You formed my inward parts; You wove me in my mother's womb.*

Jeremiah 29:11 (ESV) *For I know the plans I have for you, declares the Lord, plans for wholeness and not for evil, to give you a future and a hope.*

Romans 8:29-30 (ESV) *For those whom he foreknew he also predestined to be conformed to the image of his Son . . . And those whom he predestined he also called, and those whom he called he also justified, and those whom he justified he also glorified.*

It is critical that we understand that we have **been created with a great purpose.** Our personalities and abilities have been uniquely developed by God Himself. We are like an exquisitely designed race car that is missing the fuel. At salvation, Jesus fills us up with His power, which ignites our true purpose and design.

The Bible is clear that even before we were born, or even the world was made, God had a plan for our lives. It is mind-blowing to think that before the beginning of time, God knew our names. He loves us with an intimacy we will never understand, and that love started long before our first breath. It is easy to forget that God is limitless, has no beginning, and is unhindered by space and time.

Psalm 90:2 (NASB) *Before the mountains were born or You gave birth to the earth and the world, even from everlasting to everlasting, You are God.*

In a world that is often chaotic and random, God is an exquisite designer. Your purpose is not random because God is not random. God is perfect, He cannot do anything haphazardly. To put it bluntly, "God doesn't make junk." His plans are the plans of a proud father, who wishes to put His sons and daughters on display.

SCRIPTURAL EXAMPLES

The theme of individual destiny and purpose is found throughout Scripture. It seems that God takes great delight in announcing what He has planned for His children. We are His sons and daughters, this we must never forget. Every good earthly father speaks hopes and dreams over his children, so how much more does the living God. He is a father who is forever good, forever just, and who does not just dream or hope, but declares!

ABRAHAM

Genesis 18:17-19 (NIV) *Then the Lord said, "Shall I hide from Abraham what I am about to do? Abraham will surely become a great and powerful nation, and all nations on earth will be blessed through him. For I have chosen him, so that he will direct his children and his household after him to keep the way of the Lord by doing what is right and just, so that the Lord will bring about for Abraham what he has promised him."*

SAMSON

Judges 13:3-5 (NIV) *The angel of the Lord appeared to her and said, "You are sterile and childless, but you are going to conceive and have a son. Now see to it that you drink no wine or other fermented drink and that you do not eat anything unclean, because you will conceive and give birth to a son. No razor may be used on his head, because the boy is to be a Nazirite, set apart to God from birth, and he will begin the deliverance of Israel from the hands of the Philistines."*

JEREMIAH

Jeremiah 1:3-4 (NIV) *The word of the Lord came to me, saying, "Before I formed you in the womb I knew you, before you were born I set you apart; I appointed you as a prophet to the nations."*

JOHN THE BAPTIST

Luke 1:13-17 (NIV) *Then an angel of the Lord appeared to him, standing at the right side of the altar of incense. When Zechariah saw him, he was startled and was gripped with fear. But the angel said to him: "Do not be afraid, Zechariah; your prayer has been heard. Your wife Elizabeth will bear you a son, and you are to give him the name John. He will be a joy and delight to you, and many will rejoice because of his birth, for he will be great in the sight of the Lord. He is never to take wine or other fermented drink, and he will be filled with the Holy Spirit even from birth. Many of the people of Israel will he bring back to the Lord their God. And he will go on before the Lord, in the spirit and power of Elijah, to turn the hearts of the fathers to their children and the disobedient to the wisdom of the righteous—to make ready a people prepared for the Lord."*

PAUL

Galatians 1:15-16 (NIV) *But when God, who set me apart from birth and called me by his grace, was pleased to reveal his Son in me so that I might preach him among the Gentiles, I did not consult any man . . .*

A STRATEGIC PURPOSE

It is not just Bible characters that have a radical God-given design! It is important for followers of Jesus Christ to understand and walk in their design because it is the path to a life that can change the world. God's design for each believer is not common, or "one size fits all." World-changers are not birthed from random circumstances; they are commissioned and equipped by God for His purposes. To say that there is no one like you on the face of the earth is not flattery because it is true. God is to receive glory in this; after all, He made you. Everything and *everyone* in the kingdom of God is strategically designed and molded, by Him for Him.

2 Timothy 1:9 (NKJV) *. . . who has saved us and called us with a holy calling, not according to our works, but according to His own purpose and grace which was given to us in Christ Jesus before time began.*

Proverbs 16:4 (NASB) *The Lord has made everything for its own purpose . . .*

Proverbs 19:21 (NASB) *Many are the plans in the mind of a man, but it is the purpose of the Lord that will stand.*

1 Corinthians 12:17-19 (NASB) *If the whole body were an eye, where would the hearing be? If the whole were hearing, where would the sense of smell be? But now God has placed the members, each one of them, in the body, just as He desired. If they were all one member, where would the body be?*

Paul taught that the Church is the "body" of Christ. Each member has its own function, as Paul describes in the 1 Corinthians verse above. If we are functioning in the body of Christ without realizing our identity and design, it is easy to become confused and despondent. We are each designed to be a strategic piece of the puzzle in the Church and in God's plan. However, we can often miss this revelation because we are looking in the wrong place. We frantically look to fill a role, all the while never realizing the identity we have in Christ.

INTIMACY = EXPLOITS

Daniel 11:32 (NKJV) *but the people who <u>know</u> their God shall be strong, and carry out great exploits.*

Believers are often busy trying to please God, all the while missing out on the most important detail—knowing Him. In order for our design to be released as God has planned, our focus must be Christ. Most of us have heard the expression that "being is more important than doing," though few of us can live daily in this peace. Many times, we grit our teeth in life and determine to try harder. God is not looking for a man or woman who will work harder; He is looking for a man or woman who will believe in Him, who will share His burdens, one who will love Him.

John 6:29 (NIV) *Jesus answered, "The work of God is this: to believe in the one he has sent."*

Mark 12:29-30 (NIV) *"The most important one," answered Jesus, "is this: 'Hear, O Israel, the Lord our God, the Lord is one. Love the Lord your God with all your heart and with all your soul and with all your mind and with all your strength.*

It takes the pressure off us to know that our identity is not found in what we can accomplish. Just as we do not receive salvation based on the good things we do, so we are not chosen for our works, our skill, our good looks, or anything else. As followers of Christ, we were chosen because God, in His grace, wanted to. There is a mystery to this that we can rejoice in. So in the knowledge of God and His favor we can move forward in our design. Just as Daniel 11 states, when we know God then we will do mighty things in His kingdom—in that order.

HOW DO YOU KNOW YOUR DESIGN?

After all this discussion, you may be curious about how God personally designed you. It is time for a bit of application! When looking to answer this question, there are three main ways: The Bible, seeking the Lord yourself, and seeking the Lord within the Church.

1. The Bible.

2 Peter 1:19-21 (NKJV) *And so we have the prophetic word confirmed, which you do well to heed . . . no prophecy of Scripture is of any private interpretation, for prophecy never came by the will of man, but holy men of God spoke as they were moved by the Holy Spirit.*

Many times in the Freedom Class, people are excited about getting prophetic revelation about their design and strongholds. However, you do not need spontaneous prophetic revelation to know your identity in Christ! The Bible is thorough in revealing your design, and it is the only word of prophecy that is certain. Everything that you receive from others, or in prayer should be tested by the Scripture (2 Timothy 3:16).

Your thoughts and focus in seeking to know your design should first and foremost be built on <u>scriptural truth</u>. The Bible has numerous verses that speak to your design and identity as a follower of Jesus Christ.

It says you are:

- A child of God (1 John 3:1).
- A royal heir (Colossians 1:12, Ephesians 1:18).
- An ambassador of Christ (2 Corinthians 5:20).
- A saint (Ephesians 1:1, Colossians 1:2).
- Fully righteous in Christ (2 Corinthians 5:21).
- An enemy of the devil (1 Peter 5:8).
- And the list could go on and on . . .

In the resource section of this book we have includes what we call "The Christian's Birthright" which gives an overview of our identity in Christ. It is also essential to search the Scriptures on your own to learn about who you are, and who you can become!

Returning to your original design is about becoming more like Jesus. Paul called it "conforming to the image" of Christ (Romans 8:29). You were created in the image of God, and through Christ you become more aligned with His attributes. Learning about your original design is not about inflating your ego; rather the purpose is for Christ to reveal Himself to you. You have a mission while on this earth! It is not about you, but the glory of Christ and the gospel being unleashed through you. The right question to ask is, "Am I lining up with what the Bible says about who I am and what I can become?"

2. Seek the Lord yourself.

James 1:5 (NIV) *If any of you lacks wisdom, he should ask God, who gives generously to all without finding fault, and it will be given to him.*

Jeremiah 33:3 (NKJV) *Call to Me, and I will answer you, and show you great and mighty things, which you do not know.*

God desires that we inquire of Him on a regular basis. This can be applied to our daily lives in the decisions that we make and the way we pray—in expectation that God wants to speak. It is no different when it comes to personally seeking the Lord in your private prayer times for Him to help you understand your original design. This is all about intimacy with Christ. We need real-time personal revelation of biblical principles. It breaks us out of the mindset that God is far away when He shows up and speaks! Personal revelation from the Lord gives us specific insight into his heart for us and endears us to Him.

Seeking the Lord in your personal prayer time is so essential because it cultivates your trust relationship with Him. When God opens your heart and mind through revelation (through Scripture or by spontaneous revelation), you are transformed forever, because you met God. It is like an epiphany; a light bulb flips on inside your head. It is the difference between *information* and *transformation*. You can receive a million prayer times and encouragement from others telling you how God sees you, but until you have encountered the living God and agreed with Him, you will never move into your design. There are many champions of the faith who set out to change the world for Christ with no prodding from others. All they had was a God given passion and a call, and trusted that God would follow through on His promises.

3. Seek the Lord within the Church.

1 Timothy 1:18 (NKJV) *This charge I commit to you, son Timothy, according to the prophecies previously made concerning you, that by them you may wage the good warfare.*

1 Corinthians 14:3 (NIV) *But everyone who prophesies speaks to men for their strengthening, encouragement and comfort.*

Scripture is clear that we are to eagerly desire the gift of prophecy and the greater gifts (1 Corinthians 14:1). These are for the strengthening, encouragement and comfort of the Church, and for a greater revelation of Christ (John 15:26, 16:14). It is the Lord's desire to speak to you regarding His purposes as seen in the above verses. In this passage of Scripture, Paul encourages Timothy to fight the good fight according to the prophecies that were made about him. In the same way, you can celebrate how God can speak through other brothers and sisters in Christ to encourage you about your design.

As noted prior, we cannot depend on prophetic words to be the driving force in our lives. But at the same time, we should never despise (but rejoice in) revelation received in the Church that is in submission to church leadership and guidance. It is incredible when God speaks to you through others about things that only you and Him know. This can clarify and confirm what you have already been sensing in your heart. Seeking this type of encouragement in the Church is not focused on life direction, but on edification (building up).

WHY IS UNDERSTANDING ORIGINAL DESIGN SO IMPORTANT TO FREEDOM?

Since God has a design for our lives, surely the enemy of our soul will want to try to hinder that plan. This pattern is seen in biblical history. It is a mystery of the Scripture, but it seems that the enemy somehow knows the potential or purpose of people as individuals. This can been seen clearly in the birth stories of Moses and Jesus. Satan sought to kill them as children through the murderous plots of Pharaoh and Herod. We are no different! Satan has come to steal, kill and destroy everything in his path—especially God's people—since we are the light of Christ on the earth.

For most of us, our God-given identity has been under attack from an early age. Rarely is this identity developed. In fact, most times it has been discouraged. Most of us were not told we were "a joy to be around." Instead, we were told what was wrong with us. Growing up, did anyone tell you that you were courageous with no limit? Or were most of the comments based on everything you had done wrong? Were critical words common, instead of words encouragement? If so, an identity has been created in you that does not reflect the truth of your original design in Christ.

Take a look at the graph on the top of the next page. It gives some practical examples of how false identities are created.

The enemy has worked (through life circumstances, people, situations, and our response to them) to create an identity that is:	The Lord wants to restore us to His original design, our true identity in Jesus Christ:
Selfish and self-preoccupied.	A servant and promoter of others.
Victimized and filled with self-pity.	One who gives hope and encouragement.
Hardened and numb.	Soft-hearted and connected emotionally.
Unforgiving and bitter.	Forgiving and filled with love.
Filled with self-hatred.	One who knows they are approved of by God.
Depressed and sorrowful.	A person of contagious joy.
Introverted and shy.	Outgoing and bold.
Visionless and confused.	Clear-minded and filled with vision and direction.
Fearful and unable to trust.	Courageous and not suspicious of others.
Cautious and afraid to witness.	Bold witness with a voice that is filled with God's power.

STRONGHOLDS: OPPOSITION TO OUR DESIGN

In the next chapter we will learn more about strongholds and how they are formed in the life of a believer in Christ. Strongholds are a main weapon of the enemy to make believers ineffective in life and ministry through debilitating bondage. We are in a war, but the victory is ours in Christ! Getting rid of strongholds is about removing every obstacle between us and Christ. When these obstacles are gone, we are able to draw nearer to Jesus and can enter more fully into His design for our lives.

The enemy's plan is that we would never enter fully into our design, become complacent, and give up. We see this concept play out in the history of Israel. According to the book of Deuteronomy (1:2), it took only eleven days to get from Mount Sinai to the Promised Land. But the Scripture says that it took the Israelites forty years to reach it, and only two from the multitudes that set out from Egypt lived long enough to enter. Due to their own unbelief, the people never lived up to God's design for their nation, which was to be a "light unto the nations." They did not believe what God had spoken about their purpose. Believers today can make the same mistake as the Israelites and miss God's best through disobedience. It is better to take the eleven-day route by obeying God, than the forty-year disappointment of doing things our own way!

RECOVERING YOUR DESIGN

Judges 6:11-16 (NIV) *The angel of the Lord came and sat down under the oak in Ophrah that belonged to Joash the Abiezrite, where his son Gideon was threshing wheat in a winepress to keep it from the Midianites. When the angel of the Lord appeared to Gideon, he said, "The Lord is with you, mighty warrior." "But sir," Gideon replied, "if the Lord is with us, why has all this happened to us? Where are all his wonders that our fathers told us about when they said, 'Did*

not the Lord bring us up out of Egypt?' But now the Lord has abandoned us and put us into the hand of Midian." The Lord turned to him and said, "Go in the strength you have and save Israel out of Midian's hand. Am I not sending you?" "But Lord," Gideon asked, "how can I save Israel? My clan is the weakest in Manasseh, and I am the least in my family." The Lord answered, "I will be with you, and you will strike down all the Midianites together."

If you are anything like Gideon in this story, you may have a hard time accepting what God says about you. Many times God calls His people "mighty warriors" but they look over their shoulder wondering if He is talking to someone else. "Surely not me" you say, "God, you must be looking for someone smarter, more talented, more spiritual." Because of the circumstances in Gideon's life and his feelings of abandonment, he had lost all hope. But you serve a God who calls a "coward" in a wine press a mighty warrior. You serve the God who calls things that are not as though they were (Romans 4:17). Are you a Gideon waiting to arise? The soothing voice of Jesus speaks out your destiny. Will you listen? The accuser speaks a word of judgement, but the blood of Christ speaks a better word (Hebrews 12:24). And His word is all that matters!

APPLICATION

Closing Questions

1. What has God said about you in the Scriptures that you have difficulty receiving or believing?

2. What are the three basic ways to know your design?

3. Why is it so important to have the Lord speak to your heart concerning your design?

4. What are some false labels that people have put on you over the years? Have you believed the lie? If so, how has this affected the way you live your life?

Group Prayer Excercise

Renounce the way people have labeled you falsely. Now you want to deal with some of the ways that you have been labeled by others so that you can begin to discover your true identity. Your instructor will lead you through this prayer.

Renounce these false labels and affirm the truth of God's Word over your life.

If there are trained and trusted prayer people available, take time pray for everyone in the class, asking the Lord this question, "Lord, how do you see _____ right now?" or, "Lord, how did you create _____."

Homework

Read the article, *What is Repentance* by Catherine Booth [pg. 91]. This is a classic text on repentance.

NOTES:

STRONGHOLDS

WHAT IS A SPIRITUAL STRONGHOLD?

2 Corinthians 10:3-5 (NKJV) *For though we walk in the flesh, we do not war according to the flesh. For the weapons of our warfare are not carnal but mighty in God for pulling down **strongholds**, casting down arguments and every high thing that exalts itself against the knowledge of God, bringing every thought into captivity to the obedience of Christ.*

2 Corinthians 10:3-5 (NASB) *For though we walk in the flesh, we do not war according to the flesh, for the weapons of our warfare are not of the flesh, but divinely powerful for the destruction of **fortresses**. We are destroying speculations and every lofty thing raised up against the knowledge of God, and we are taking every thought captive to the obedience of Christ.*

In a literal physical sense, a stronghold serves as a military camp, a fortified defense (for a territory), a base of operations, or a headquarters. A spiritual stronghold works in a very similar way to a material one. A stronghold is made up of sin expressed in a person's thoughts, beliefs, attitudes, philosophies, actions, and values that oppose the truth of God. Strongholds are a "launching pad" for enemy influence in our lives.

Example: *If one nation is plotting to take over another nation, they will try and set up a stronghold on the opposition's soil. This way, troops and supplies can be launched from this base. It is the same with the enemy: he wants a place of operation in our lives so that he can expand his influence.*

HOW IS A SPIRITUAL STRONGHOLD BUILT?

Strongholds are built by allowing the enemy to have a place or opportunity in our lives through sin. The Greek word **topos** is translated place, opportunity, or foothold in the Ephesians 4:27. It is a word with broad meaning, but it is fundamentally defined as: "territory, land: in the oldest clear use in the singular it means a defined place." [1]

Ephesians 4:26-27 (NKJV) *"Be angry, and do not sin." Do not let the sun go down on your wrath, nor give **place** to the devil.*

Ephesians 4:26-27 (NASB) *Be angry and yet do not sin; do not let the sun go down on your anger, and do not give the devil an **opportunity**.*

Ephesians 4:26-27 (NIV) *"In your anger do not sin." Do not let the sun go down while you are still angry, and do not give the devil a **foothold**.*

Example: *Even though followers of Jesus Christ belong to God, they can give the enemy a place, or jurisdiction in their lives. It is like driving a car: You do not have to have the title to a car to drive it; all you need is the key. With that key, you can drive anywhere you please. So it is with Satan. A Christian forever belongs to God (with an impenetrable spirit), but if we give the enemy jurisdiction in an area of our lives, he will certainly take us for a ride!*

THE PROGRESSION OF A STRONGHOLD

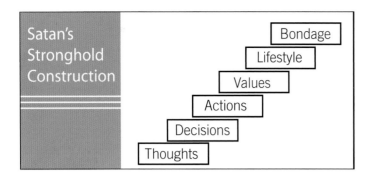

LOOKING BEYOND BEHAVIOR

When we speak of sin issues (whether ours or others') we often focus on outward behavior. Behavior comes from the overflow of our heart—from the state of our inner being (Luke 6:45). Our behavior will always flow from our inner heart, whether for sin or righteousness. When seeking to remove strongholds, **we must get to their roots**. Like the tree graphic on the next page, if we only cut off the leaves or the branches, they will grow back. But if the **tree is cut at the roots**, it will fall.

The next three illustrations will help us to visualize strongholds and how they are built.

Case # 1	Case # 2	Case #3
Abuse *(Injustice/Root)*	Abandonment *(Injustice/Root)*	Rejection *(Injustice/Root)*
Fear *(Lie/Stronghold)*	Self-Hatred *(Lie/Stronghold)*	Unforgiveness *(Lie/Stronghold)*
Control *(Behavior)*	Pornography *(Behavior)*	Anger *(Behavior)*

Strongholds are not built overnight. They are built progressively as we agree with the enemy, starting with our thoughts and ending in bondage (as the above graphic shows). As we read in 2 Corinthians 10, a stronghold is described as *any speculation, argument, or thought that raises itself up against the knowledge of God*. We allow lies to go unchecked in our lives, which gives access to the enemy. This is why Paul states that our new life in Christ begins with the renewing of our minds.

Romans 12:2 (NLT) *Don't copy the behavior and customs of this world, but let God transform you into a new person by changing the way you think. Then you will know what God wants you to do, and you will know how good and pleasing and perfect his will really is.*

It is by dwelling on thoughts that we make decisions; our decisions become actions, and these soon become our life values. These values begin to define who we are and eventually become our lifestyles. When our thoughts are out of alignment with God's truth, our lifestyle is in opposition to God. We then find ourselves in varying degrees of bondage as Satan builds his strongholds in our lives. But the blame does not lie with the enemy. The old adage "the devil made me do it," is unbiblical and is a shifting of responsibility. He builds strongholds through obtaining a place of jurisdiction that you have personally invited through disobedience.

Example: *A man commits adultery. He did not just wake up one morning and decide to be unfaithful to his wife. It was a progression of months and maybe years. It probably started with a glance at a woman who was not his wife. The glance became a decision to let his mind wander, and not take his thoughts captive. He then acted on that decision through viewing ungodly images just one time (pornography). The one time becomes a few times. The few times eventually becomes a habit, a value. Pretty soon the man becomes numb to his besetting sin and becomes unsatisfied with his wife. His conscience is seared and his lifestyle begins to shift as he slowly has given into lie after lie. This ends in the bondage of adultery and the rejection of godly wisdom.*

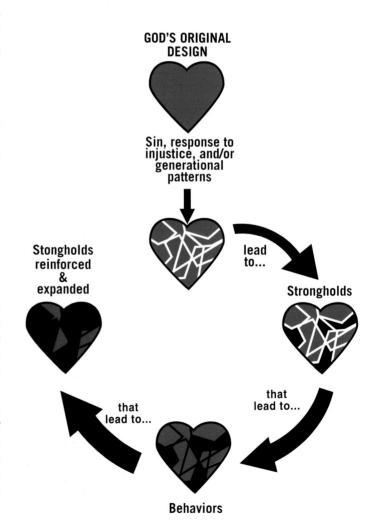

GOD'S ORIGINAL DESIGN

Sin, response to injustice, and/or generational patterns

lead to...

Strongholds

that lead to...

Behaviors

that lead to...

Strongholds reinforced & expanded

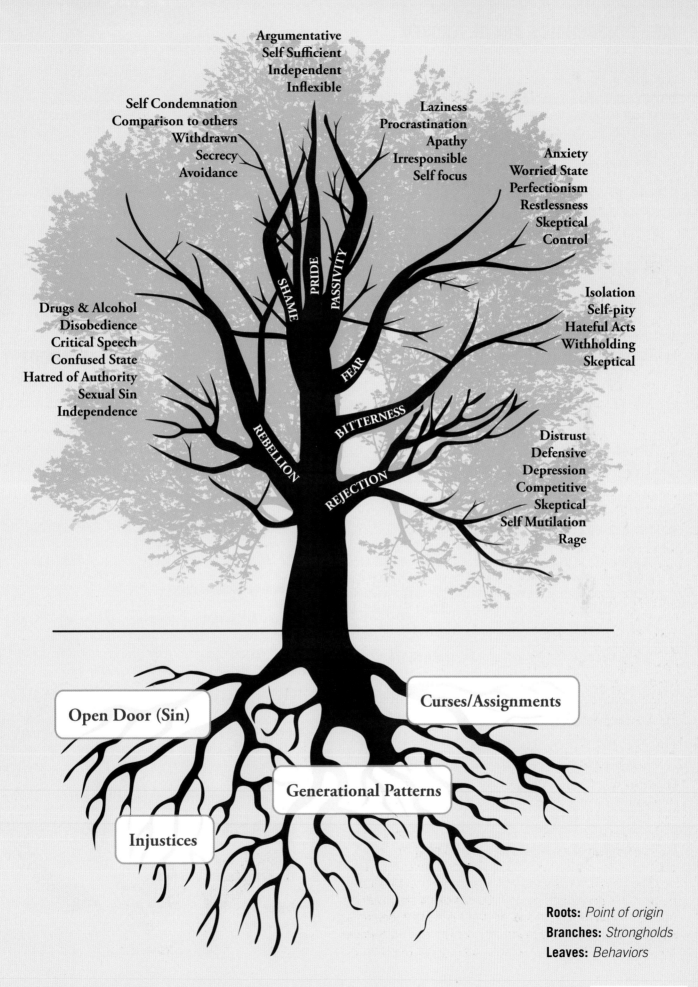

Argumentative
Self Sufficient
Independent
Inflexible

Self Condemnation
Comparison to others
Withdrawn
Secrecy
Avoidance

Laziness
Procrastination
Apathy
Irresponsible
Self focus

Anxiety
Worried State
Perfectionism
Restlessness
Skeptical
Control

Drugs & Alcohol
Disobedience
Critical Speech
Confused State
Hatred of Authority
Sexual Sin
Independence

Isolation
Self-pity
Hateful Acts
Withholding
Skeptical

Distrust
Defensive
Depression
Competitive
Skeptical
Self Mutilation
Rage

SHAME
PRIDE
PASSIVITY
FEAR
BITTERNESS
REBELLION
REJECTION

Open Door (Sin)

Curses/Assignments

Generational Patterns

Injustices

Roots: *Point of origin*
Branches: *Strongholds*
Leaves: *Behaviors*

HOW STRONGHOLDS ARE DESTROYED

2 Corinthians 10:4 tells us that we have **divinely powerful weapons** for the destruction of strongholds. We have already exercised some of these weapons practically in this class. For the sake of clarity, we will review how to destroy strongholds.

1. The weapon of truth.

It begins and ends with truth. The foundation of a sin stronghold is an absence or distortion of God's truth. John 14:6 tells us that Jesus is "the way the truth and the life." The Scriptures are the truth of God in written form. The Scriptures expose and correct every area of our life that is not aligned with God's truth. This is why we must saturate ourselves in the Scriptures through reading, listening, teaching, meditation, and memorization.

2. The weapon of Jesus Christ's authority.

We learned about this weapon in the next chapter. Nothing can stand up to Jesus' authority. This authority is fully ours—we just need to walk it out in faith!

3. The weapon of repentance.

This weapon is so powerful that Satan has nothing in his arsenal that can stand against it.

4. The weapon of forgiveness.

Forgiveness is a two-edged sword: Sometimes we must grant forgiveness for what people have done to us and for the injustices we have suffered; other times we need to ask for forgiveness from God or others because we have sinned against them.

5. The weapons of prayer and spoken declarations.

Spoken words are very powerful. In chapter six we will learn that the power of life and death exists in spoken words. When we pray and declare something in faith and conviction, a spiritual transaction occurs. Just as there are business transactions that can affect our earthly lives, so there are spiritual transactions that do the same. When we speak forth a declaration in Christ's authority that is based on God's truth, powerful spiritual transactions occur.

6. The weapon of a humble and obedient life.

This is the end product of tearing down strongholds. A life characterized by humility and obedience toward God is a mighty weapon. We need the heart of Christ.

DESTROYING STRONGHOLDS IS ABOUT THE CONDITION OF OUR HEART

1. A heart of humility.

James 4:6 (NLT) *He gives us more and more strength to stand against such evil desires. As the Scriptures say, "God sets Himself against the proud, but He shows favor to the humble."*

James 4:10 (NLT) *When you bow down before the Lord and admit your dependence on Him, He will lift you up and give you honor.*

2. A heart of submission.

James 4:7-9 (NIV) *Submit yourselves, then, to God . . . Come near to God and he will come near to you. Wash your hands, you sinners, and purify your hearts, you double minded. Grieve, mourn and wail . . .*

3. A heart of confession and repentance.

James 4:8-9 (NIV) *Wash your hands, you sinners, and purify your hearts, you double minded. Grieve, mourn and wail...*

4. A heart of aggressive resistance to Satan.

James 4:7 (NIV) *Submit yourselves, then, to God. Resist the devil . . .*

5. The promise: He will flee!

James 4:7 (NIV) *. . . Resist the devil, and he will flee from you.*

THE GIFT OF REPENTANCE

The foundational truth in destroying strongholds in our life is repentance. Repentance is not morbid introspection and ungodly sorrow. Contrary to popular opinion, repentance is a wonderful and privileged *gift given to us by God*. This is apparent in the following verses:

Acts 5:29-31 (NKJV) . . .*God exalted him to his own right hand as Prince and Savior that He might **give repentance** and forgiveness of sins to Israel.*

Acts 11:18 (NKJV) . . .*Well then, **God has granted** to the Gentiles also the repentance that leads to life.*

2 Timothy 2:25 (NASB) . . .*Those who oppose Him He must gently instruct, in the hope that **God will grant** them repentance leading them to a knowledge of the truth . . .*

Romans 2:4 (NASB) *Do you think lightly of the riches of His kindness and tolerance and patience, not knowing that the kindness of God **leads you** to repentance?"*

REVISITING TRUE REPENTANCE

Repentance is not merely being convicted of sin. We can be convicted over sin but never change our hearts or activities. We can hear a sermon about how being critical and spreading gossip is sin. We can reach personal conviction about the damage these sins cause—without making a life change. We continue to live exactly as we did before. That is not repentance.

Repentance is not simply sorrow over sin. We can cry days of tears over a particular area of sin that God is exposing and still not be repentant. We are simply sad because we were found out. It would be like a bank robber crying over getting caught instead of mourning that he shot the bank teller to get the money. There are tears, but no heart change. He is crying over what has been lost but has no joy over what has been gained through true repentance.

New Song City Central (Tacoma, WA) pastor, Brian Brennt, tells this story of a young man and an issue of repentance:

A man came forward at New Song for the better part of a year asking for prayer each night to overcome a pornography addiction. He would often complain that the Lord was not assisting him in change and thus would continually ask for prayer. Finally, one night, I told the man that he had never truly repented once of his pornography, and that is why his struggles persisted. He could not believe it and became angry with me. I told him to go home and throw away his computer, all of his magazines, and to drive a different way to work so as to avoid temptation. "Do whatever it takes to respond to God," I said. "Move in with brothers who will hold you accountable. Throw away your TV and pour yourself into the Word of God." The man became silent and looked at me and said, "This I cannot do'" and walked out the back of the church with tears in his eyes.

THE TRUE MEANING OF REPENTANCE

- The Greek word scholars translate as repentance in the verses on the previous page is *metanoia*. It literally means "a change of mind." True repentance is filled with radical implications, for it turns us *from* something, *toward* something *different*.

- Repentance transforms your life, your values, your attitudes, and your actions. True biblical repentance includes your entire being: the mind, will, and emotions. This results in new thoughts and beliefs, new words and actions, and eventually new emotions.

- It is *not enough to be sorrowful for sin*; you must change your values, belief systems, and lifestyle in order to make specific changes to turn from sin. It is important to note that repentance is an ongoing process.

The chart below shows from Scripture what repentance looks like. This is taken from Ephesians 4:25-32.

VERSE	UNRIGHTEOUS BEHAVIOR TO ABANDON	RIGHTEOUS BEHAVIOR TO EMBRACE
25	Lying.	Speak only truth.
28	Stealing from others.	Work to be able to give away.
29	Unwholesome, abusive talk.	Words that build up others, and minister grace to others, appropriate to the time.
31-32	Bitterness, rage, anger, harsh words, slander, and hostile behavior.	Tenderhearted kindness, forgiving others as Christ has forgiven you.

TO REPENT YOU:

1. STOP SINNING AND CONFESS YOUR SIN

1 Corinthians 15:34 (NIV) *Come back to your senses as you ought, and stop sinning . . .*

1 John 1:9 (NIV) *If we confess our sins, he is faithful and just and will forgive us our sins and purify us from all unrighteousness.*

2. TURN FROM YOUR SIN

2 Timothy 2:19 (NIV) . . . *Everyone who confesses the name of the Lord must turn away from wickedness.*

3. DO THE OPPOSITE

Ephesians 4:28 (NIV) *He who has been stealing must steal no longer, but must work, doing something useful with his own hands, that he may have something to share with those in need.*

REAL POWER, NOT MERE WORDS

1 Corinthians 4:20 (NIV) *For the kingdom of God is not a matter of talk but of power.*

Jesus Christ did the work of forgiveness on the cross. There is a transaction that happens in the spiritual realm when you become a Christian. And this power grows as you walk in obedience to Him. This transaction has far reaching ramifications. As you look at the process of living in God's original design and freedom it is important to remember that you need Holy Spirit empowerment!

YOU NEED THE POWER OF GOD!

1. You cannot receive freedom from self-help or positive thinking.
2. You cannot earn freedom or strive for it.
3. Sheer human will cannot bring lasting change.
4. You cannot wish away your bondage.
5. Trying to "figure out" how to change will fail.
6. <u>There must be a spiritual transaction!</u>
7. You must cry out to God in desperate need!

PRAYING REPENTANCE
THE "4-R's" AND SUPPORTING SCRIPTURES

1. **REPENT** of the sin.
   Call it what it is. It is your sin. It may be a heart attitude, like bitterness, rebellion, or pride. It could be a behavior, like alcohol abuse, immorality, or stealing. It could even be a feeling, like rejection, inferiority, or shame. (Note: In the instance of abuse or wounding, the initial sin is not yours. That is not your fault. Your sin is your response: anger, fear, unforgiveness, bitterness, shame, etc. Recognize this sin and confess it!)

   Acts 3:19 (NIV) *Repent, then, and turn to God, so that your sins may be wiped out, that times of refreshing may come from the Lord.*

2. **RECEIVE** God's forgiveness and cleansing.
   Ask God to fill you anew with His Holy Spirit; to strengthen you in your thoughts, behavior, and emotions.

   Psalm 103:8-12 (NIV) *The LORD is compassionate and gracious, slow to anger, abounding in love. He will not always accuse, nor will He harbor His anger forever; He does not treat us as our sins deserve or repay us according to our iniquities. For as high as the heavens are above the earth, so great is His love for those who fear Him; as far as the east is from the west, so far has He removed our transgressions from us.*

   1 John 1:9 (NIV) *If we confess our sins, He is faithful and just and will forgive us our sins and purify us from all unrighteousness.*

3. **REBUKE** the enemy's hold on you because of this sin.
   Take your rightful place of authority through the power of Jesus' death and resurrection and renounce any comfort or "payoff" received from this sin.

   Matthew 4:10 (NIV) *Jesus said to him, "Away from me, Satan!"*

   James 4:7 (NIV) *Submit yourselves, then, to God. Resist the devil, and he will flee from you.*

4. **REPLACE** all lies with God's TRUTH!
   Declare old attitudes, actions, and emotions dead and "paid for." Fill your heart and mind with TRUTH that is consistent with the character of Jesus Christ and God's Word. Walk out your repentance with action. Ask the Holy Spirit to guide and empower you to do it!

   Galatians 2:20 (NIV) *I have been crucified with Christ and I no longer live, but Christ lives in me. The life I live in the body, I live by faith in the Son of God, who loved me and gave himself for me.*

   Ephesians 5:18 (NIV) *" …be filled with the Spirit."*

BONUS: OPEN DOORS . . .

When we sin, we allow the enemy an "open door" to our lives. The term "open door" refers to specific "topos," or jurisdiction, that have been opened that day or week to the enemy through sin. Examples of open doors are: passivity, self-pity, anger, lying, gossip, and being critical. The term "open door" means that you have opened the door to sin during the day.

1. How do you close an open door?

A person identifies where the door was open to sin and walks through the 4-R's. Ask the Lord to show how many doors you have opened to sin that day. Then confess the sins that He reveals.

2. How often do you pray about open doors?

Pray each day and seek the Lord for areas in which you opened the door. This is the beginning of a lifestyle of repentance. The purpose is not to be introspective and self degrading, but to pray with the heart of David in Psalm 139:23, "Search me, O God, and know my heart; test me and know my anxious thoughts." Pray each day and seek the Lord for areas in which you opened the door. This is the beginning of a lifestyle of repentance.

3. What if I have the same open door every day?

This is common when you begin your restoration. However, the greater the repentance, the less you will confess the same area. It is important to ask the Lord for a hatred of sin so that you can break quickly out of lifelong stronghold patterns.

4. What if I am married?

When you come into agreement over the importance of closing doors of sin, you can do this together as a married couple. It is good to make a habit of closing the day with prayer in this manner.

5. Do I teach my children how to pray this way?

Yes, start with the 4-R's. Take the class on Marriage and Freedom, which explains more about how to walk as a family in restoration.

(ENDNOTES)

1. *Theological Dictionary of the New Testament* (10 Vols.) G. Kittel, G. W. Bromiley and G. Friendrich, Ed. (Grand Rapids: Erdmans, 1964-1976).

APPLICATION

Closing Questions

1. What (in your own words) is a spiritual stronghold, and where do you find this concept in Scripture?

2. What (in your own words) is a foothold or "topos," and where do you find this concept in Scripture?

3. Why is repentance so essential to the destruction of strongholds?

4. What are the 4-R's? Why are these concepts so important in prayer?

5. In the destruction of a stronghold, why is it so important to get to the root and not just merely try to change behaviors?

Stronghold Worksheet

Practice tearing down strongholds together in class!
Use the 4-R's as a tool to lead you through. Each stronghold worksheet has a sample prayer at the end to help you in the process. There is no "formula" prayer; these are just to help with the general principles in the truth of God's Word. The key is not the right *words* but your *heart* of humble obedience and submission to Christ.

This session's worksheet: *Fear* [pg. 60]
Fear will try to rob you of your confidence in Christ and your ability to receive His love. Your instructor will lead you in combatting this enemy scheme.

Homework

In preparation for the next class, read *Breaking Free, Part 1* [pg. 93]. This is an introduction to the authority that you are given in Christ.

NOTES:

AUTHORITY OF THE BELIEVER

4

CARRYING OUT JESUS' MINISTRY REQUIRES JESUS' AUTHORITY AND POWER

In order to flourish in all God has planned for His Church, and for us as individuals, we must learn to use the authority He has given us. It is the difference between a toy gun and a bazooka. When we come to minister, we do not come in our own power and authority. What can we do to change anything? As most of us have probably experienced, we are powerless to preach, love, heal, or do any effective ministry on our own. Nothing good comes from our own ideas and abilities alone. Flesh cannot overcome the impossible, but with God, ALL things are possible (Mark 10:27). We should never come in our own name, but in the name of Jesus. He has all the power and authority, and *we have none*. Therefore, we need His authority and His power to do His work. This changes the way we view just about every area of our lives! Paul makes it clear in 1 Corinthians 4 that the kingdom of God is not about great words, but real power.

1 Corinthians 4:19-20 (NIV) *But I will come to you very soon, if the Lord is willing, and then I will find out not only how these arrogant people are talking, but what power they have. For the kingdom of God is not a matter of talk but of power.*

Acts 1:8 (NLT) *But when the Holy Spirit has come upon you, you will receive power and will tell people about Me everywhere in Jerusalem, throughout Judea, in Samaria, and to the ends of the earth.*

THE DISTINCTION BETWEEN AUTHORITY & POWER

While God's authority and power are inseparably related, there is a distinct difference between them. Jesus was identified as having God's authority and power; likewise, Jesus gave both authority and power to His disciples.

Luke 4:36 (NIV) *All the people were amazed and said to each other, "What is this teaching? With **authority and power** He gives orders to evil spirits and they come out!"*

Luke 9:1 (NIV) *He called the twelve together, and gave them **power and authority** over all the demons, and to heal diseases.*

DEFINING THE DIFFERENCE BETWEEN AUTHORITY AND POWER

1. **Authority is the <u>right</u> to rule.**

   Authority is based upon given position, and this position gives that person the right to rule within the limits and scope of a designated authority.

   ILLUSTRATION: *A police officer has authority in his precinct as defined by the government of the land. But he would not have any authority to police people in other cities or countries. Likewise, the officer could not march into a battalion headquarters on a military base and start directing soldiers. That would be outside his or her realm of authority.*

2. Power is the <u>ability</u> to rule.

God extends His power to believers to exercise His authority on earth, to continue His ministry. This is why He gave it to His disciples, as we read in Luke 9; and it is why, at His ascension, He instructed the disciples and the 120 not to go out and do ministry until they received God's power from heaven. Every believer in Jesus Christ has His extended authority, but *many do do not use their authority in power.* So the resource is available, yet lies dormant!

Luke 24:47-49 (NLT) *It was also written that this message would be proclaimed in the authority of his name to all the nations, beginning in Jerusalem: "There is forgiveness of sins for all who repent.'" You are witnesses of all these things. "And now I will send the Holy Spirit, just as my Father promised. But stay here in the city until the Holy Spirit comes and fills you with power from heaven."*

CHRIST'S AUTHORITY IS ULTIMATE AND IS THE SOURCE OF OUR AUTHORITY

Ephesians 1:19-22 (NASB) *. . .These are in accordance with the working of the strength of His might which He brought about in Christ, when He raised Him from the dead, and seated Him at His right hand in the heavenly places, far above all rule and authority and power and dominion, and every name that is named, not only in this age, but also in the one to come. And He put all things in subjection under His feet, and gave Him as head over all things to the church. . . And God raised us up with Christ and seated us with him in the heavenly realms in Christ Jesus.*

Ephesians 1:3 (NASB) *Blessed be the God and Father of our Lord Jesus Christ, who has blessed us with <u>every spiritual blessing</u> in the heavenly places [heavenlies realm] in Christ.*

No one and no thing has greater power or authority than Jesus. God has placed all things under Jesus' feet and Satan cannot stand against Jesus' authority. The "every spiritual blessing" that is mentioned in Ephesians 1:3 does not mean the spiritually "warm and fuzzy" feeling we get while listening to a favorite worship album. The blessings described are spiritual resources, capacities, weapons, and gifts that are not a part of our personalities or natural abilities. These blessings can only come from God Himself. They include our position in Christ and our weapons in Christ—both of which allow us to operate in the heavenlies (the spiritual realm). *Being "in Christ" is the key that opens these spiritual blessings up to us. The foundation is understanding our authority in Christ.*

JESUS MINISTERED IN & UNDER AUTHORITY AND SO SHOULD WE

Not only did Jesus marvel and respond to people who understood and lived in authority, He also lived a life in and under authority Himself. Though Jesus was fully God, He still lived a life of submission to authority as a man. The Gospels demonstrate that He lived under the authority of His father as well as human authorities. If we want to move in the power and authority of God, we must follow in the footsteps of Christ by walking in obedience to God and His delegated authorities. If we cannot submit to the authority of appointed authorities in our lives, how can we submit to God?

John 5:30 (NLT) *But I do nothing without consulting the Father. I judge as I am told. And my judgment is absolutely just, because it is according to the will of God who sent me; it is not merely my own.*

John 7:16 (NLT) *So Jesus told them, "I'm not teaching my own ideas, but those of God who sent me."*

John 8:26; 28 (NLT) *I have much to say about you and much to condemn, but I won't. For I say only what I have heard from the one who sent me, and he is true. So Jesus said, "When you have lifted up the Son of Man on the cross, then you will realize that I am he and that I do nothing on my own, but I speak what the Father taught me."*

John 12:49-50 (NLT) *I don't speak on my own authority. The Father who sent me gave me his own instructions as to what I should say. And I know his instructions lead to eternal life; so I say whatever the Father tells me to say!*

Matthew 22:17-21 (NLT) *"Now tell us what you think about this: Is it right to pay taxes to Caesar or not?" But Jesus knew their evil motives. "You hypocrites!" he said. "Why are you trying to trap me? Here, show me the coin used for the tax." When they handed him a Roman coin, he asked, "Whose picture and title are stamped on it?" "Caesar's," they replied. "Well, then," he said, "give to Caesar what belongs to Caesar, and give to God what belongs to God."*

Matthew 17:27 (NLT) *However, we don't want to offend them, so go down to the lake and throw in a line. Open the mouth of the first fish you catch, and you will find a large silver coin. Take it and pay the tax for both of us.*

Matthew 9:6; 8 (NLT) *"I will prove that I, the Son of Man, have the authority on earth to forgive sins." Then Jesus turned to the paralyzed man and said, "Stand up, take your mat, and go on home, because you are healed!" Fear swept through the crowd as they saw this happen right before their eyes. They praised God for sending a man with such great authority.*

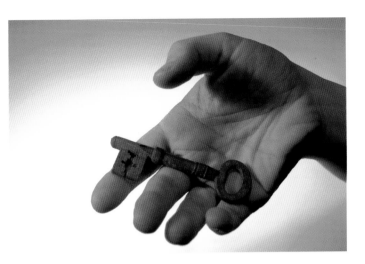

JESUS GIVES HIS AUTHORITY TO US

It is obvious to us that Christ had authority from God. He was, after all, God incarnate. It is also easily understood from Scripture that the disciples were given the authority and power to do the very things Jesus was doing. But are we to continue on in this same authority even today—continuing the ministry of Jesus? Is there biblical precedent to believe that we have been given this same authority?

1. **The twelve disciples received Christ's authority.**

   Luke 9:1 (NLT) *One day Jesus called together his twelve apostles and gave them power and authority to cast out demons and to heal all diseases.*

2. **The seventy-two disciples received Christ's authority.**

   Luke 10:1, 17-19 (NLT) *The Lord now chose seventy-two other disciples and sent them on ahead in pairs to all the towns and villages he planned to visit ...When the seventy-two disciples returned, they joyfully reported to him, "Lord, even the demons obey us when we use your name!" "Yes," he told them, "I saw Satan falling from heaven as a flash of lightning! And I have given you authority over all the power of the enemy, and you can walk among snakes and scorpions and crush them. Nothing will injure you.*

3. **All of us have received Christ's authority.**

   In Jesus' prayer to the Father in John 17, he prays for His disciples and everyone who would ever believe in Him because of their message. That is us! If you are a follower of Jesus Christ, then you are one of His disciples. You might not be one of the original twelve (neither were the seventy-two listed above who received His authority), but you believe because their message has traveled through the generations from person to person—and finally to your ears.

Jesus makes it clear in this text that we are sent into the world as He was, with the same authority and mission. John 14 states Jesus says that "anyone" who has faith in Him will actually do even greater things than He. This is a startling revelation and an amazing mission we get to share in.

John 17:18, 20-21 (NLT) *As you sent me into the world, I am sending them into the world. I am praying not only for these disciples but also for all who will ever believe in me because of their testimony. My prayer for all of them is that they will be one, just as you and I are one, Father— that just as you are in me and I am in you, so they will be in us, and the world will believe you sent me.*

John 14:12-13 (NIV) *I tell you the truth, anyone who has faith in me will do what I have been doing. He will do even greater things than these, because I am going to the Father. And I will do whatever you ask in my name, so that the Son may bring glory to the Father.*

Matthew 28:18 (NLT) *Jesus came and told his disciples, "I have been given complete authority in heaven and on earth. Therefore, go and make disciples of all the nations, baptizing them in the name of the Father and the Son and the Holy Spirit. Teach these new disciples to obey all the commands I have given you. And be sure of this: I am with you always, even to the end of the age."*

Matthew 16:19 (NIV) *I will give you the keys of the kingdom of heaven; whatever you bind on earth will be bound in heaven, and whatever you loose on earth will be loosed in heaven.* (Keys represent authority)

WE RECEIVE THIS AUTHORITY AT SALVATION

Ephesians 2:4-6 (NASB) *But God, being rich in mercy, because of His great love with which He loved us, even when we were dead in our transgressions, made us alive together with Christ (by grace you have been saved), and raised us up with Him, and seated us with Him in the heavenly places, in Christ Jesus. . .*

- Ephesians 2:1-3 tells us that we used to be under the dominion of hell, Satan, and his minions.

- Jesus, the great Savior, came and delivered us from the dominion of Satan and transferred us into His kingdom.

- Jesus not only delivered us from Satan's domain, but He swept us up and seated us with Him in the heavenlies (Ephesians 1:19-22).

- This is a present reality, not one that will be realized only in the future. We now possess every spiritual blessing in the heavenlies (Ephesians 1:3).

THE AUTHORITY STRUCTURE OF THE WORLD

Colossians 2:9-10 (NIV) *For in Christ all the fullness of the Deity lives in bodily form, and **you have been given fullness** in Christ, who is the head over every power and authority.*

Hebrews 2:14 (NASB) *Therefore, since the children share in flesh and blood, He Himself likewise also partook of the same, that through death He might **render powerless** him who had the power of death, that is, the devil, and might free those who through fear of death were subject to slavery all their lives.*

Colossians 2:13-15 (NIV) *When you were dead in your sins and in the uncircumcision of your sinful nature, God made you alive with Christ. He forgave us all our sins, having canceled the written code, with its regulations, that was against us and that stood opposed to us; he took it away, nailing it to the cross. And **having disarmed the powers and authorities**, he made a public spectacle of them, triumphing over them by the cross.*

This chart shows the authority structure of the world:

UNBELIEVER	BELIEVER
Jesus Christ Ephesians 1:22	Jesus Christ Ephesians 1:22
	Believers Ephesians 2:6
Satan Ephesians 2:2	Satan Ephesians 2:2
Spirits Luke 13:11	Spirits Luke 13:11
Human Beings Genesis 1:26	Human Beings Genesis 1:26
Animals Psalms 8:6-8	Animals Psalms 8:6-8

REMEMBER THAT YOU ARE A "CERTAIN" DISCIPLE OF CHRIST

So many times we default to thinking we are disqualified as instruments of God's demonstrated power because we are just "normal" people. We could never be a Peter, John, or Paul, let alone even consider being an Elijah or Moses. However, James negates any potential for deifying these men by letting us know that Elijah was a normal human being just like us.

James 5:17 (NASB) *Elijah was a man <u>with a nature like ours</u>, and he prayed earnestly that it would not rain, and it did not rain on the earth for three years and six months.*

The Scripture does not hide the "warts" of men and women in biblical accounts. Abraham had his messy days as a human being; as did Moses, King David, and the Apostle Peter. We are not any different. God does not release His power to do strategic and supernatural things in perfect human beings, for there are none! He uses His imperfect children!

Look at the Scripture about a man named Ananias in the book of Acts:

Acts 9:10-11 (NKJV) *Now there was a certain disciple at Damascus named Ananias; and to him the Lord said in a vision, "Ananias." And he said, "Here I am, Lord." So the Lord said to him, "Arise and go to the street called Straight, and inquire at the house of Judas for one called Saul of Tarsus, for behold, he is praying."*

Acts 9:17-18 (NKJV) *And Ananias went his way and entered the house; and laying his hands on him he said, "Brother Saul, the Lord Jesus, who appeared to you on the road as you came, has sent me that you may receive your sight and be filled with the Holy Spirit." Immediately there fell from his eyes something like scales, and he received his sight at once; and he arose and was baptized.*

The New King James Version describes Ananias as a "certain" disciple. We never hear of him again. We do not read that Ananias had a high position or office in the early church. He simply was a "certain" disciple through whom God exercised His mighty power. God used Ananias to impart healing to Saul and the filling of God's Spirit for his amazing life and ministry. You qualify as a "certain" disciple if you are, through His grace, a believing follower of Jesus Christ.

JESUS I KNOW, PAUL I KNOW, BUT WHO ARE YOU?

Acts 19:13-16 (NIV) *Some Jews who went around driving out evil spirits tried to invoke the name of the Lord Jesus over those who were demon-possessed. They would say, "In the name of Jesus, whom Paul preaches, I command you to come out." Seven sons of Sceva, a Jewish chief priest, were doing this. One day the evil spirit answered them, "Jesus I know, and I know about Paul, but who are you?" Then the man who had the evil spirit jumped on them and overpowered them all. He gave them such a beating that they ran out of the house naked and bleeding.*

The seven sons of Sceva thought they could simply use the name of Jesus and the demons would flee—they were wrong! Authority is not about saying the right thing; it is about who you know. The sons of Sceva did not believe in Christ, so they had no authority—they were not authorized to use His name. They were all then beat to a bloody pulp by one man! But when we move in the power and authority of Christ, (like Paul) the enemy knows our name because we are followers of Jesus Christ.

APPLICATION

Closing Questions

1. What is the difference between power and authority? Why is the distinction important?

2. Why is it important to be under (submitted to) human authority in order to move in Christ's authority?

3. How does John 17:18-21 help you understand your mission to continue the ministry of Christ?

4. As a follower of Christ, when do you receive His authority?

5. As a believer, what authority do you have over the powers of the enemy? Do you have to be specially gifted in this area, or do all believers have this authority?

Stronghold Worksheet

Practice using your authority together in class! When we come against the enemy we can come in confidence. It is in the name and authority of Christ that we are victorious. Come before the Lord with great privilege of repentance, and with a fierceness rebuke the enemy.

This session's worksheet: *Passivity* [pg. 63]
Passivity is a lethargy of spirit that will hinders our use of Christ's authority. Passivity says that we do not need to get radical in our devotion to Christ. Passivity is always comfortable and never wants to be challenged . . . it is time to get rid of it!

Homework

In preparation for the next class, read *Breakthrough in Discipline* [pg. 96]. This assignment gives practical pointers on areas of discipline in which you continually want to grow.

NOTES:

NOTES:

EFFECTS OF INJUSTICE

5

UNDERSTANDING INJUSTICE

One of the core ways that strongholds can be built in our lives is through our reaction to unjust life circumstances. These reactions can be either aggressive or passive, but they lead to the same result—bondage. Injustice is best defined as *unmerited harm*. We realize that we did nothing to deserve the treatment that was given, and nothing can be done to change what happened. Injustice is grievous to God and angers Him greatly, as it is the opposite of His justice and is foreign to His character.

Deuteronomy 32:4 (NASB) *The Rock! His work is perfect, for all His ways are just; A God of faithfulness and without injustice, righteous and upright is He.*

But unlike God, we very rarely can have righteous anger over injustice or anything else in our lives. We react to injustice primarily in anger, bitterness, unforgivingness, withdrawal, or other sin patterns. Simply put, **an injustice provokes the construction of strongholds.**

Many times we assume that because we were wronged, we have the right to take offense and to retaliate in word, action, or bitterness. This is not the heart of Christ, and even in Christian ministry it is inevitable that all of us will be affected by overt injustice. In addition, all of us have suffered under less overt (but no less hurtful) injustices from childhood forward. In order to live in the freedom of Christ, we must confront these injustices and our reactions to them. In doing so, we can grant full forgiveness to all who have caused suffering or rejected us.

TRUTH AND LOVE DEFICITS

Any relationship or situation in our lives that does not reflect the full truth or love of God is an opportunity for the enemy to build strongholds. The injustice of not receiving a purity of love and truth allows this access. This is the principle of *love and truth deficits*. Wherever there is a deficit of love or truth, the empty space will be filled with lies. Let us look at how love and truth deficits practically play out in our lives.

1. Truth deficit.

God's truth brings peace and fruitfulness to our lives. The degree to which we stray from this truth is the degree to which we can be controlled by varying strongholds (2 Corinthians 10:3-5). If truth is withheld, unhealthy and destructive patterns grow. Here are a few examples:

Rebellion:
A child determines when he will listen to his parents. He has selective obedience and is rarely corrected by his parents, who do not instruct him to obey out of fear of rejection from their child. There is no instruction in the godly character of patience, listening, or obedience. Thus, the child simply will not listen to his parents, doing what he wants, when he wants. As an adult, this lack of truth affects every relationship and environment of his life, including how he sees God, church authorities, employers, etc. The man thinks he is autonomous and does not need the help or instruction of anyone. Out of this comes confusion, anger, offense, chaos, and anarchy in varying degrees.

Unforgiveness:

A young woman is abused verbally by her mother at an early age. Her mother is bitter because her husband left her, and takes out the frustration about her situation on her little girl. The mother harbors bitterness and unforgiveness toward the father. Soon the daughter learns that being bitter and angry in the house is alright. This girl grows up with deep unforgiveness toward her father, mother, and others, and sees no problem with it.

Note: The absence of truth has deep and far-reaching ramifications. The greater the number of truth deficits, the greater and more far-reaching is the damage to a person's life. There is never just one arena where truth is absent; therefore the damage becomes complex.

2. **Love deficit. (Deprivation of "God-quality" love)**

Just as with a truth deficit, a love deficit can cause unhealthy and destructive patterns in our lives. As much as well-meaning (and potentially godly) people in our lives love us, they will never measure up to God's perfect standard of love. When this standard is not met, the result can be damaging:

Withholding:

A young girl is seldom, if ever, told she is loved. True, genuine, unconditional, godlike love is seldom, if ever, demonstrated to this girl. Even worse, there is outright neglect, disregard, and rejection. She is abandoned mentally, emotionally, physically, and relationally. She seldom hears the truth of God's unconditional love and regard for her. In fact, she hears the exact opposite: She is not good enough, she is ugly, and she is average.

Performance-based Relationships:

A man believes that his worth is equal to his performance. This value was ingrained in him by his father who would give love based on his son's performance. He was never told he had inherent worth or that he would be loved no matter what he did. Later in life the son tries hard to please those around him by doing everything "just right" in an attempt to win approval. He soon experiences the pain of rejection, because his performance does not always measure up to those around him.

3. **Being loved is essential for spiritual health.**

Love is central to our development!

- God is love, and expresses His love to us relationally.
- We are created to love Him and be loved.
- Others' words and actions express love and blessing.
- We question our value when love is not expressed to us.

Love and truth deficits affect our identity:

- Love is related to value and worth. The more love deficits people experience in their lives, the less valuable and worthy they feel.
- If love is absent, it leaves a lack of significance and security.
- Lack of love results in real or perceived rejection.
- It develops patterns of trying to capture love and significance, and/or an unnatural desire to protect ourselves from the hurt of rejection.
- This is especially significant in the developmental years of life where lifelong patterns are built.
- We will often try to fill a void of love through performance, striving, unhealthy addictions, independence, or other "replacements" for love.
- It becomes more difficult for us to see these issues because they become such a part of daily lives and personalities.
- Deficits, and the strongholds built because of them, are more quickly identified by others through revelation and observation than by the person themselves.

OUR REACTION TO LOVE AND TRUTH DEFICITS

When love and truth is withheld from us, we will often respond in one of two ways: passively or aggressively. How we respond is determined by our make-up as a person. The enemy is never satisfied, nor stagnant in his efforts against God's creation, kingdom, people, and Church. He is out to steal, kill, and destroy absolutely everything. He will use the injustice of love and truth deficits to provoke us to passive or aggressive sin patterns.

Here are some examples of how we can respond to the injustice and rejection of love and truth deficits. These are examples of the progression of sin the enemy wants to start.

Passive

Passivity, insecurity, inferiority, apathy, depression, condemnation, victimization, hopelessness, self-hatred, etc., that *eventually lead to suicide.*

Aggressive

Rebellion, jealousy, pride, control, superiority, competition, criticism, hostility, bitterness, anger, rage, etc., *that eventually lead to murder.*

The Progression of an Injustice...

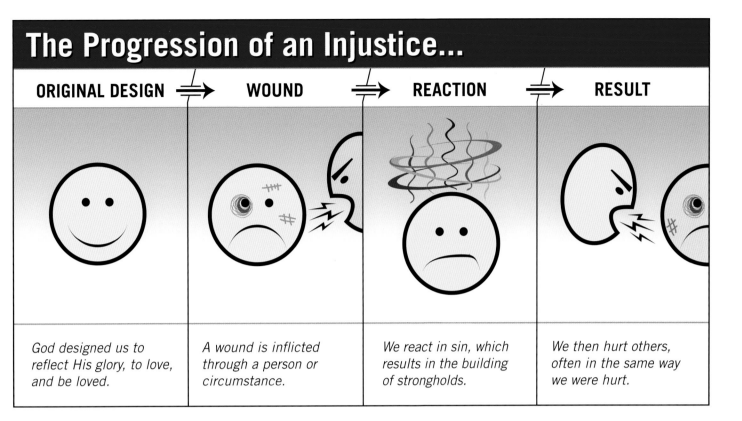

ORIGINAL DESIGN ⇒	WOUND ⇒	REACTION ⇒	RESULT
God designed us to reflect His glory, to love, and be loved.	*A wound is inflicted through a person or circumstance.*	*We react in sin, which results in the building of strongholds.*	*We then hurt others, often in the same way we were hurt.*

EXAMPLES OF INJUSTICE

As much as we want to avoid ever encountering an injustice in our lives, they are unavoidable in a fallen world. Some injustices are subtle and develop over time, while other forms are flagrant events that can leave us disheartened and hopeless for the future.

It is common for individuals to suffer from an injustice and never recognize it. The injustice has become so much a part of life, that it seems normal. Then there are situations where someone suffers a severe betrayal from a friend, and then act like it did not affect them, all the while seething with anger and bitterness deep inside. We cannot ignore past injustice and act like nothing happened. The avoidance does nothing but harm us further because it solidifies the enemy's hold.

Common types of injustice include:

- Rejection.
- Betrayal by a close friend.
- Divorced parents.
- Addicted parents.
- Physical or verbal abuse.
- Unfulfilled promises.
- False accusation.
- Misunderstandings.
- Manipulation or control (domination).
- Withholding.

OUR SIN REACTION

Suffering from an injustice is not a sin (since by its very definition it is unjust), but our reaction to an injustice can be sinful. As stated prior, an injustice can provoke the construction of strongholds. Injustice, and the likely offense response that follows, is like bait set to snare us in sin. If we choose to take the bait, we react to the injustice in sin, for which we alone are responsible. In the Christian life, it does not matter who or what comes against us; we <u>never</u> have the right to take offense. No matter how unjust the situation, if we receive the offense (through anger, bitterness, isolation, etc.), we are held accountable for that sin.

Some common reaction patterns of injustice:

- Victim mentality: everything in our lives that goes wrong is then blamed on a past injustice.
- Becoming angry with God: "Where was God when . . ."
- Distrust of others: people must prove themselves beyond a healthy measure.
- Grumbling, complaining, and thanklessness.
- Gossip, backbiting, and territorialism.
- A desire for vengeance: "I hope they get what is due them . . . then they will learn."
- Disengaging socially and emotionally from others.
- Reluctance to take risks, speak out, be bold, try new things, trailblaze new ministries, etc.

CAN WE BECOME UNOFFENDABLE?

Luke 17:1 (NKJV) *Then He said to the disciples, "It is impossible that no offenses should come, but woe to him through whom they do come!*

The word for offenses in Luke 17:1 can be translated, *temptations to sin, stumbling blocks, things that cause people to sin, occasions for stumbling, etc.* Jesus makes it clear that there will always be the temptation to take offense, or to react in sin. While injustices can be unavoidable, we are not helpless against such attacks. The best way to overcome an injustice is to never let offense take root in our hearts. Injustice loses its power when we do not succumb to its provoking. And if we do succumb, we can have victory by relinquishing our offense through repentance and forgiveness.

Our goal is to be like Christ, who suffered under intense injustice in its purest form and yet did not retaliate:

1 Peter 2:19-21 (NIV) *For it is commendable if a man bears up under the pain of unjust suffering because he is conscious of God. But how is it to your credit if you receive a beating for doing wrong and endure it? But if you suffer for doing good and you endure it, this is commendable before God. To this you were called, because Christ suffered for you, leaving you an example, that you should follow in his steps. "He committed no sin, and no deceit was found in his mouth." When they hurled their insults at him, he did not retaliate; when he suffered, he made no threats. Instead, he entrusted himself to him who judges justly. He himself bore our sins in his body on the tree, so that we might die to sins and live for righteousness; by his wounds you have been healed.*

2 Corinthians 5:21 (NASB) *He made Him who knew no sin to be sin on our behalf, so that we might become the righteousness of God in Him.*

Christ took the punishment for sin that He never committed. Jesus was accused of being demon possessed, yet He was the very son of God. Christ was called a madman by His own family. He was betrayed by His closest friends. He was rejected by all the religious leaders of His own people. The list could go on and on. If anyone had the right to be outraged, angry, bitter, and calloused, it was Jesus! Yet His heart was always, "Father, forgive them; for they know not what they do" (Luke 23:34, KJV). This is the same heart God desires for us, and it is not impossible for us to forgive in this way or God would not require it.

Luke 6:27-29 (NASB) *But I say to you who hear, love your enemies, do good to those who hate you, bless those who curse you, pray for those who mistreat you. Whoever hits you on the cheek, offer him the other also . . .*

1 Thessalonians 5:15 (NASB) *See that no one repays another with evil for evil, but always seek after that which is good for one another and for all people.*

If we sense an offense is trying to take root in our lives, through the power of the Holy Spirit we must immediately forgive those who have hurt us and allow God to bring justice. In this way we get to share in the excitement and passion of becoming more like Christ!

GOD IS VICTORIOUS AND REDEEMS SUFFERING

Romans 8:28 (NASB) *And we know that God causes **all things to work together for good** to those who love God, to those who are called according to His purpose.*

Genesis 50:19-20 (NASB) *But Joseph said to them, "Do not be afraid, for am I in God's place? As for you, you meant evil against me, but **God meant it for good** in order to bring about this present result, to preserve many people alive."*

God is never the author of injustice, but He can use something that was meant for evil and turn it for good. This is not a cliché; it is the truth of God found throughout Scripture. Whatever way suffering comes, God can and will use it for His own glory. As stated in the *Original Design* section of this book, God's desire is for us to be conformed to the image of Christ (Romans 8:29). This process is always costly, and is continuous until we see Him face to face. So while injustice is not God's plan, it can be used by Him to form Godly character, and in the end produce a great harvest for His kingdom.

1 Peter 4:12-13 (NIV) *Dear friends, do not be surprised at the painful trial you are suffering, as though something strange were happening to you. But rejoice that you participate in the sufferings of Christ, so that you may be overjoyed when his glory is revealed.*

The story of Joseph's life is a key example of this principle. He was rejected and hated by his brothers, sold into slavery, and imprisoned—yet he had done nothing to deserve such wicked treatment. Like us, Joseph needed to relinquish the past and receive God's healing. This release is described in Genesis:

Genesis 41:51-52 (NLT) *Joseph named his older son Manasseh, for he said, "God has made me <u>forget</u> all my <u>troubles</u> and the family of my father." Joseph named his second son Ephraim, for he said, "God has made me <u>fruitful</u> in this land of my suffering."*

Manasseh means "to forget." [1] Just as God allowed Joseph to forget the troubles of his past injustice, so we can be renewed in the power of Christ to forget our past and move forward in victory.

Joseph named his second son Ephraim, for he said, "God has made me fruitful in this land of my suffering." Ephraim means: "I shall be doubly fruitful." [2] This name speaks of the restoration, hope, and healing that occurred in Joseph's life. God's restoration and healing comes as we live in obedience to Him and forgive those who have harmed us.

God uses affliction to prompt repentance; for example, the purpose of the wilderness wandering was to humble Israel (Deuteronomy 8:2). This is a recurring theme in Scripture. God was not the author of the suffering in Joseph's life, but the Lord used the training that came because of it: Joseph's godly character was developed. This can be the result of injustice in our lives, if we allow the Lord to do His work.

PRACTICAL STEPS TO BREAKING THE HOLD OF INJUSTICE

1. Identify a past injustice.

First identify the injustice and agree that it was not your fault (this disarms the lie that you deserved the treatment). Some injustices you can identify yourself, while others you might need revelation from the Lord. Some tools you can use as a catalyst include the *Rejection Worksheet* and the *Anger Worksheet*. These tools may help identify specific types of past injustices.

2. Forgive and bless everyone who harmed you.

The key point of breakthrough is when you forgive everyone who participated in the injustice. Be specific in your forgiveness and your blessing. The injustice could be a deep wound and it may be very difficult to forgive. But through the power of the Holy Spirit you can forgive them just as Christ has forgiven you. Remember, forgiving someone is not declaring that what they did was right. The *Unforgiveness Worksheet* can help you through this process.

3. Ask forgiveness for <u>your reaction</u> to the injustice.

Ask the Lord to forgive you for your specific sin reactions to the injustice, whether it be anger, unforgiveness, withdrawal, etc. Use the 4-R's to help in this process [pg. 23]. One common reaction that needs to be dealt with is anger toward God.

4. Release the right to understand why the injustice happened.

This is a key step. You no longer need to know why this injustice occurred. God can and will have victory through (or in spite of) all that has happened.

5. Declare release and healing from your past!

As you release your past, ask the Lord to exchange it for a "Mannaseh" and "Ephraim." This means asking the Lord for a deep healing of all the pain and declaring that it is a new day. His love is so deep for you, let it penetrate . . .

(ENDNOTES)

1. Strong, J. 1996. Enhanced Strong's Lexicon (H5382). Woodside Bible Fellowship: Ontario.
2. Ibid.

APPLICATION

Closing Questions

1. In your own words, what is an injustice?

2. How do love and truth deficits build strongholds in your life? Why are love and truth deficits injustices?

3. What are common sin reactions to an injustice? Can you recognize some of these reactions in your own life?

4. What is the best way to overcome an injustice? How did Christ model this for us?

5. Throughout the teaching, what specific instances of an injustice in your own life came to mind? Ask the Lord to give you further revelation and begin the process of forgiveness and repentance as described on page 35.

Stronghold Worksheet

What good would it be to learn about injustice, yet not remove the effects of it in our own lives? Injustice is a huge inroads for the enemy, and needs to be taken seriously. The *Rejection Worksheet* will help you start the process of identifying injustice in your life, and the *Unforgiveness Worksheet* will help lead you through the process of forgiveness.

This session's worksheets: Your instructor will lead you through the *Rejection* and *Unforgiveness* Worksheets [pg. 67-73, 79-84].

Homework

Thoroughly work through the *Anger Worksheet* in the Stronghold Worksheet section of the book [pg 53]. Do not rush the process of prayer. It is best to pray through this with a trusted friend.

NOTES:

BLESSINGS & CURSES

6

+definition+

CURSE:

[noun] 1) a calling on God or the gods to send evil or injury down on some person or thing. 2) a blasphemous oath; 3) a thing cursed. 4) evil or injury that seems to come in answer to a curse. [1]

[verb] 1) to utter a wish of evil against; to imprecate evil upon, to call injury down on, to execrate. . . 3) to afflict; to subject to evil; to blight with a curse; to bring evil or injury on. [2]

[According to James 3] curses are words toward others that diminish, slander, dishonor, discourage, and are often based out of jealousy, envy, competition, and striving.

BLESS:

[verb] *1) to hallow or consecrate by religious rite or word . . . 3) to invoke divine care . . . 5) to confer prosperity or happiness upon.* [3]

[According to James 3] *are words toward others that build up, strengthen, encourage, honor, and are grace and faith based.*

THE REALITY OF CURSES

In a recent newsletter, the relief organization *Food for the Hungry* (dated July 2002) had a front page article titled, "Breaking the Spell of Witchcraft." The following is an excerpt from that article. *"Witch-doctors and curses may seem the stuff of Hollywood movies. But unfortunately, for much of the world, belief in the supernatural has power over people's lives. In Gorongosa, Mozambique, the power of witchcraft is so strong that it is listed as the second leading cause of death. The witch-doctors have even formed an organization that governs their beliefs. Because witchcraft is an accepted part of the community, fighting demonic powers and the fear caused by the witch-doctors is difficult. Pastors teaching the Word of God are harassed, even threatened with death."*

Especially among Christians, curses are regarded as something purely mystical, make-believe, or the subject of fairy tales. We cannot base our understanding only on what we have personally experienced—we must ask the question, "What does the Bible say about curses?" How many of us have been blinded to the biblical truth regarding curses and are actually living plagued by them?

This is not to suggest that curses are the cause of everything adverse in our lives, or that dealing with curses will be the solution for all our problems. We just need to be wise in dealing with subjects of spiritual significance and always remember that what is going on "behind the scenes" can have a real effect on our physical lives.

Zondervan Pictorial Encyclopedia of the Bible states this about curses: *Primitive people believed that one could pronounce a curse on his enemy and that deity or superhuman beings could be enlisted to execute it. By this means, all kinds of disaster, sickness, or hardship could be inflicted . . . Indeed, the validity of pronounced blessings and the antithesis of cursing in early Bible history is amazing. Noah pronounced a curse on Canaan, and a blessing on Shem and Japheth (Genesis 9:25-27), and subsequent history confirmed his invocations . . . A curse was a characterized entity, a power, force, or energy expressing itself in hurt to be feared and shunned . . . A curse was not considered a mere wish for misfortune on one's enemies, but a potent force capable of translating pronouncements into tangible results.* [2]

BLESSINGS AND CURSES AND THE POWER OF THE TONGUE

James 3:6 (NLT) *It [the tongue] is full of wickedness that can ruin your whole life. It can turn the entire course of your life into a blazing flame of destruction, for it is set on fire by hell itself.*

James 3:9-10 (NLT) *Sometimes [the tongue] praises our Lord and Father, and sometimes it breaks out into curses against those who have been made in the image of God. And so blessing and cursing come pouring out of the same mouth. Surely, my brothers and sisters, this is not right!*

Proverbs 18:21 (NIV) *The tongue has the power of life and death, and those who love it will eat its fruit.*

1. **Western culture trivializes the power of the spoken word.**

   You know the famous proverb of Western culture, *"sticks and stones may break my bones but words will never hurt me."* Completely false!

   Is it possible that many Christians are beleaguered by unbroken curses on their lives, and the lives of their families? Is it possible that there is much heartache, tension, adversity, sorrow, and ills upon Christians due to the work of curses on their lives? In the same way, spoken blessings carry a spiritual significance and power. How would the lives of our loved ones change if we fully unleashed Christ-like blessing upon them?

2. **Words are powerful.**

   God brought the world into existence with the spoken word. He spoke, and out of nothing the world was formed.

Psalm 33:6 (NLT) *The Lord merely spoke, and the heavens were created. He breathed the word, and all the stars were born.*

Hebrews 11:3 (NASB) *By faith we understand that the worlds were prepared by the word of God, so that what is seen was not made out of things which are visible.*

3. **The Scriptures speak of two realms: the invisible (heavenlies) and the visible (natural) realms. Words affect change in the spiritual realm.**

   We cannot see with our natural eyes the effects of our words, but they can cause change in the spiritual realm. For greater learning on this subject please read the article in the back of the book titled *Our World Has Two Realms*, pg. 86.

BLESSINGS & CURSES APPEAR THROUGHOUT THE SCRIPTURES

Blessings and curses are mentioned over **640 times** in the Scriptures. Here are a few examples:

<u>JOSHUA'S CURSE</u>
Joshua 6:26 (NASB) *Then Joshua made them take an oath at that time, saying, "Cursed before the Lord is the man who rises up and builds this city Jericho; with the loss of his firstborn he shall lay its foundation, and with the loss of his youngest son he shall set up its gates."*

1 Kings 16:34 (NLT) *It was during his reign that Hiel, a man from Bethel, rebuilt Jericho. When he laid the foundations, his oldest son, Abiram, died. And when he finally completed it by setting up the gates, his youngest son, Segub, died. This all happened according to the message from the Lord concerning Jericho spoken by Joshua son of Nun.*

- The fulfillment took place 500 years after Joshua spoke the curse.

JESUS' DISCIPLES AND APOSTLES

Luke 10:5-6, 8-11 (NLT) *"Whenever you enter a home, give it your blessing. If those who live there are worthy, the blessing will stand; if they are not, the blessing will return to you. If a town welcomes you, eat whatever is set before you and heal the sick. As you heal them, say, 'The Kingdom of God is near you now.' But if a town refuses to welcome you, go out into its streets and say, 'We wipe the dust of your town from our feet as a public announcement of your doom. And don't forget the Kingdom of God is near!'"*

- Shaking dust off from the feet is symbolic of pronouncing a curse.
- Pronouncing a blessing brought real natural world blessing; to retract the blessing would take away real natural world blessing.

THE APOSTLE PAUL

Acts 13:9-12 (NASB) *But Saul, who was also known as Paul, filled with the Holy Spirit, fixed his gaze on him, and said, "You who are full of all deceit and fraud, you son of the devil, you enemy of all righteousness, will you not cease to make crooked the straight ways of the Lord? Now, behold, the hand of the Lord is upon you, and you will be blind and not see the sun for a time." And immediately a mist and a darkness fell upon him, and he went about seeking those who would lead him by the hand. Then the proconsul believed when he saw what had happened, being amazed at the teaching of the Lord.*

SOME TRUTHS ABOUT BLESSINGS AND CURSES

1. **Blessings and curses can be generational.**

    Genesis 28:2-4 (NLT) *May God Almighty bless you and give you many children. And may your descendants become a great assembly of nations! May God pass on to you and your descendants the blessings he promised to Abraham. May you own this land where we now are foreigners, for God gave it to Abraham.*

    2 Timothy 1:5 (NIV) *I have been reminded of your sincere faith, which first lived in your grandmother Lois and in your mother Eunice and, I am persuaded, now lives in you also.*

    Deuteronomy 30:19 (NIV) *This day I call heaven and earth as witnesses against you that I have set before you life and death, blessings and curses. Now choose life, so that you and your children may live.*

ISRAEL'S PRIESTLY BLESSING

Numbers 6:22-27 (NASB) *Then the Lord spoke to Moses, saying, "Speak to Aaron and to his sons, saying, 'Thus you shall bless the sons of Israel. You shall say to them: The Lord bless you, and keep you; The Lord make His face shine on you, and be gracious to you; The Lord lift up His countenance on you, And give you peace.' So they shall invoke My name on the sons of Israel, and I then will bless them."*

BALAK'S REQUEST FOR BALAAM TO CURSE THE PEOPLE

Numbers 22:6,12 (NASB) [Balak the king of Moab's message to Balaam] *Now, therefore, please come, curse this people for me since they are too mighty for me; perhaps I may be able to defeat them and drive them out of the land. For I know that he whom you bless is blessed, and he whom you curse is cursed . . .* [God's response to this request] *God said to Balaam, "Do not go with them; you shall not curse the people, for they are blessed."*

- This example shows us the reality and seriousness of pronouncing curses.

ELISHA TOWARD GEHAZI

2 Kings 5:25-27 (NLT) *When he went in to his master, Elisha asked him, "Where have you been, Gehazi?" "I haven't been anywhere," he replied. But Elisha asked him, "Don't you realize that I was there in spirit when Naaman stepped down from his chariot to meet you? Is this the time to receive money and clothing and olive groves and vineyards and sheep and oxen and servants? Because you have done this, you and your children and your children's children will suffer from Naaman's leprosy forever." When Gehazi left the room, he was leprous; his skin was as white as snow.*

- Gehazi received judgment by the spoken word curse of Elisha.

2. **The Christian's responsibility regarding blessings and curses.**

   Luke 6:28 (NASB) *Bless those who curse you, pray for those who mistreat you.*

   Romans 12:14 (NASB) *Bless those who persecute you; bless and do not curse.*

   1 Corinthians 4:12 (NLT) *We have worked wearily with our own hands to earn our living. We bless those who curse us. We are patient with those who abuse us.*

   1 Peter 3:9 (NASB) *Not returning evil for evil or insult for insult, but giving a blessing instead; for you were called for the very purpose that you might inherit a blessing.*

THE FOUNDATION FOR BEING RELEASED FROM A CURSE—THE DEATH AND RESURRECTION OF CHRIST

The great truth is that Jesus bore everything related to sin and death so that we might have righteousness and life.

1. **Jesus became our sin so we could receive His righteousness.**

   2 Corinthians 5:21 (NASB) *He made Him who knew no sin to be sin on our behalf, so that we might become the righteousness of God in Him.*

2. **Jesus was wounded so we could be healed.**

   Isaiah 53:4-5 (NIV) *Surely he took up our infirmities and carried our sorrows, yet we considered him stricken by God, smitten by him, and afflicted. But he was pierced for our transgressions, he was crushed for our iniquities; <u>the punishment that brought us peace was upon him, and by his wounds we are healed</u>.*

3. **Jesus became poor so that we might become rich.**

   2 Corinthians 8:9 (NIV) *For you know the grace of our Lord Jesus Christ, that though he was rich, yet for your sakes he became poor, so that you through his poverty might become rich.*

4. **Jesus bore our shame so that we might obtain His glory.**

   Hebrews 12:2 (NASB) *. . . fixing our eyes on Jesus, the author and perfecter of faith, who for the joy set before Him endured the cross, despising the shame, and has sat down at the right hand of the throne of God.*

   Hebrews 2:10 (NASB) *For it was fitting for Him, for whom are all things, and through whom are all things, in bringing many sons to glory, to perfect the author of their salvation through sufferings.*

5. **Jesus became a curse so we could receive the blessing.**

   Galatians 3:13-14 (NASB) *Christ redeemed us from the curse of the Law, having become a curse for us—for it is written, "Cursed is everyone who hangs on a tree"— in order that in Christ Jesus the blessing of Abraham might come to the Gentiles, so that we would receive the promise of the Spirit through faith.*

PRACTICAL STEPS FOR RELEASE FROM LIVING UNDER CURSES

1. Salvation: Be assured you have eternal life in Jesus Christ—the foundation for overcoming all sin and power(s) of darkness.

2. Repent of all known sin, accept forgiveness, and confess that you submit every aspect of yourself and life to God—especially sins that exposed you to curses (include generational sins and curses).

3. Confess and repent of all known sin you have committed against others (make necessary restitution), including words of death (curses) you spoke against them, and sever all word curses. Speak blessings to replace the curses.

4. Forgive all who have wronged or violated you and bless them.

5. Renounce all interest or activity in anything occultic or anything that gives honor to Satan's kingdom.

6. In faith and conviction, pray a prayer of release from any and every curse by the blood of Jesus Christ.

7. In faith and conviction pray that God will loose His blessing(s), particularly speak blessings that replace a specific curse(s).

LIVING A LIFE-STYLE OF RELEASE FROM CURSES AND WALKING IN BLESSINGS

1. **Seek forgiveness for words of death you have spoken.**

   - Identify who you have spoken words of death toward (words that tear down and not build up, words that are critical) and what the words were.

   - It is important to break the specific words of death you spoke toward others as you remember them.

   - After the words and ways have been identified and spoken, and you have asked forgiveness from God for speaking such words, then simply state something such as: *"I sever the power of these words of death against _____ in the name of Jesus Christ, and by the blood of Jesus Christ and the power of His resurrection, I rebuke all evil spirits who energize those words, and command you to be gone and go before Jesus."*

   - Then speak words of life (blessing) toward the person.

   Possible persons you may have spoken a curse toward:
   - Parents and/or siblings.
   - Spouse and/or children.
   - Spiritual authority figures in a church and/or ministry.
   - Other Christians.
   - Particular churches or denominations.
   - Authority figures at school, work, or government.
   - Work associates.
   - God.
   - Friends.
   - Yourself.

2. **Sever the curses that have come against you from yourself, others, and previous generations.**

   Possible areas to consider:
   - Spiritual poverty.
   - Health (curses of illness).
   - Finances (curses of poverty).
   - Marriage (unity and intimacy).
   - Family breakdown.
   - Fruitful and abundant ministry.
   - Curses that enforce strongholds (sins) of life.
   - Confusion and disunity.
   - Curses from occult influence (games, literature, music, etc.).

   Luke 11:36 (NLT) *If you are filled with light, with no dark corners, then your whole life will be radiant, as though a floodlight is shining on you.*

   They can be self-inflicted curses:
   - I am stupid . . .
   - I can never be like . . .
   - I will always be poor . . .
   - I can never do that . . .
   - I am rejected and lonely . . .
   - Singing lyrics to songs that are words of self-destruction.

(ENDNOTES)

1. Webster's New Twentieth Century Dictionary Of the English Language, ed. Jean L. McKechnie, (William Collins and World Publishing Company; 1977).
2. Ibid.
3. "rebellion." *Merriam-Webster Online Dictionary.* 2007. http://www.merriam-webster.com (11 Jan. 2007).
4.. Merrill C. Tenney, ed., The Zondervan Pictorial Encyclopedia of the Bible, (Grand Rapids; Zondervan , 1975).

APPLICATION

Closing Questions

1. How does the book of James describe the power of the tongue?

2. If someone curses you, what is your response to be as a Christian?

3. What are some common "words of death" that you have spoken over yourself or others? Take the time to ask for forgiveness and break the power of those words.

4. What words of blessing have you withheld from your loved ones? What practical changes are you going to make in how you speak to others and how you bless them?

Group Prayer Declaration

In your time with the Lord this week make sure you thoroughly pray through the section titled "Practical steps for Release from Living Under Curses" [pg.40]. Do not be paranoid about curses; simply be aware of their reality and respond biblically.

Stronghold Worksheet

This session's worksheet: *Shame* [pg. 74]
Shame always makes it seem like you are alone in your struggles. Break its power!

Homework

As a follow-up to this class, read *Our World Has Two Realms* by Mike Riches [pg. 86]. This is a great overview that can deepen your understanding of the world in which we live and the heavenlies realm.

NOTES:

INTERCESSION & BREAKING GENERATIONAL PATTERNS

7

This lesson can change your life forever! Take the time to press in and learn everything you can about the powerful work of intercession.

JESUS IS OUR MODEL FOR INTERCESSION

Romans 8:34 (NIV) *Who is he that condemns? Christ Jesus, who died—more than that, who was raised to life—is at the right hand of God and is also **interceding** for us.*

It is clear in Scripture that Christ is constantly interceding for His children. So Jesus is praying for you right now. He is our ultimate example for intercession and having a heart-cry for salvation and change in others. Intercession is praying on behalf of another. In order to pray for someone with conviction, we must be able to *identify* with them.

Identification is one of the deep roots of intercession. Jesus' identification with us is so intense that we can have a hard time understanding its depth. Think about what Jesus went through while on earth: He went through everything we do and more. Not only does He identify with us and our struggles, He literally took our place as our sin and sickness bearer on the cross. Jesus understands us because He became us—but He was without sin.

Think about the many ways Jesus identified with us:
- He experienced loneliness.
- He experienced persecution.
- He experienced betrayal.
- He experienced injustice.
- He experienced pain.
- He had His heart broken.
- He was misunderstood.
- He was homeless and poor.
- He knew what it meant to work hard.
- He had a job (carpenter).
- He was a child.
- He was a teenager.
- He was hated.
- He experienced sorrow.
- He faced hard and costly decisions.
- He faced opposition.
- He understood rejection.
- He was treated disrespectfully and people made fun of him.
- He was accused falsely.
- He was lied to.
- He knew what it meant to love someone and have them accuse Him of wrongdoing.
- He knew what righteous anger felt like.
- He understood the pain of losing loved ones.
- He knew the pain of being mocked and spat upon.
- He knew what it meant to be ignored and mistrusted.

INTERCESSION: STANDING IN THE GAP

Hebrews 7:25 (NIV) *Therefore he is able to save completely those who come to God through him, because he always lives to intercede for them.*

Isaiah 59:16 (NKJV) *He saw that there was no man, and wondered that there was no intercessor; therefore His own arm brought salvation for Him.*

We see in the above verse, in Isaiah, that God was looking for an intercessor. He was looking for someone to "stand in the gap." If God was *looking* for someone to intercede, we get a sense of just how rare a true intercessor is, because there was *no one* to stand in the gap. Intercession is a prayer in which we generously give our all. We give our heart and soul; we give our "guts!" In this passage of Scripture, the prophet Isaiah wrote that God could find no intercessor, so He sent His own son Jesus Christ.

Isaiah then wrote that Jesus identified with our sin. He bore the sin of the world; He stood in the gap so that we could be free!

Isaiah 53:12 (NKJV) *Therefore I will divide Him a portion with the great, And He shall divide the spoil with the strong, Because He poured out His soul unto death, And He was numbered with the transgressors, And He bore the sin of many, And made intercession for the transgressor.*

Isaiah 52:13-15 (NIV) *See, my servant will act wisely; he will be raised and lifted up and highly exalted. Just as there were many who were appalled at him—his appearance was so disfigured beyond that of any man and his form marred beyond human likeness—so will he sprinkle many nations, and kings will shut their mouths because of him. For what they were not told, they will see, and what they have not heard, they will understand.*

Read chapter 53 of Isaiah tonight after class. To what depth did Christ identify with us?

QUALITIES OF AN EFFECTIVE INTERCESSOR

Certain qualities make us effective intercessors:

1. **A spirit of submission.**

    Yielding to the Lord's will is our heart. We must align ourselves with God, not only in areas of holiness, but in all areas of obedience. We must submit to His order, His timing, and His plan. To submit is to yield control, and to "come under." In times of war, a soldier "submits" to his commanding officer.

    Matthew 6:9-10 (NIV) *This, then, is how you should pray: "Our Father in heaven, hallowed be your name, your kingdom come, your will be done on earth as it is in heaven."*

2. **Live in unity and agreement.**

    The book of Acts uses an interesting phrase several times in reference to believers in Christ: Being in "one accord." One accord means to run together in unity. In order for the Spirit of God to be unleashed in our midst , we must be in *agreement*. There is *real power* in it. God is repelled by division. The enemy thrives on division: he loves envy, strife, and all forms of gossip.

    We are going *nowhere* without a spirit of agreement! Think of unity as the fuel of a healthy prayer life. Without that fuel, we are stuck in one place! The heart of an intercessor is to agree with others for breakthrough.

+definition+

INTERCESSION

1: the act of interceding
2: prayer, petition, or entreaty in favor of another

IDENTIFICATION

1a: an act of identifying: the state of being identified **1b:** evidence of identity **2a:** psychological orientation of the self in regard to something (as a person or group) with a resulting feeling of close emotional association [1]

Matthew 18:18-19 (NIV) *"I tell you the truth, whatever you bind on earth will be bound in heaven, and whatever you loose on earth will be loosed in heaven. Again, I tell you that if two of you on earth agree about anything you ask for, it will be done for you by my Father in heaven. For where two or three come together in my name, there am I with them."*

3. Move in the spirit of faith.

We cannot come to God and expect Him to respond, if we do not believe He will. It is simple, but true. We foster faith in our own lives by obeying God through the trials of life, trusting that He will come through on His promises. We want to create an atmosphere in our churches and homes that practically yells "FAITH!" To be an intercessor, we must believe for the impossible.

Hebrews 11:6 (NIV) *And without faith it is impossible to please God, because anyone who comes to him must believe that he exists and that he rewards those who earnestly seek him.*

James 1:6-8 (NIV) *But when he asks, he must believe and not doubt, because he who doubts is like a wave of the sea, blown and tossed by the wind. That man should not think he will receive anything from the Lord; he is a double-minded man, unstable in all he does.*

4. Move in a spirit of persistence.

Intercessors moved by the spirit of God never give up. They might get knocked back, discouraged and weary, but they will not give up. There are a couple of key components to moving in a spirit of persistence:

a. Intercessors are driven by truth, not emotions.

When we intercede for someone or something, we cannot look at the natural realm to judge the prayer's effectiveness. We see with eyes of faith because we know the Word of God; we believe in the character of God and His promises. In the Christian life, we move in faith, not by sight. We must be grounded by the word of God.

Example:
In 1999, John F. Kennedy Jr. was fatally wounded in a mysterious plane accident. One compelling theory is the fact that John Jr. had never learned to fly his six-seater Piper Saratoga 32 by the instruments. It was a hazy night with barely any moonlight. He only flew **by sight**, became disoriented, and misjudged his location.

b. "Give him no rest."

If there is one thing that God loves, it is to be "bothered" by intercessors. We must break the lie that God has "better things to do" than listen to our prayers. God loves you with an undying love! He loves you to come to Him with your own needs and the needs of others. He is moved by our faith and our persistence. The concept of persistence is found throughout the scriptures and in the parables of Jesus.

Isaiah 62:6-7 (NIV) *I have posted watchmen on your walls, O Jerusalem; they will never be silent day or night. You who call on the LORD, give yourselves no rest, and give him no rest till he establishes Jerusalem and makes her the praise of the earth.*

Luke 18:1-8 (NIV) *Then Jesus told his disciples a parable to show them that they should always pray and not give up. He said: "In a certain town there was a judge who neither feared God nor cared about men. And there was a widow in that town who kept coming to him with the plea, 'Grant me justice against my adversary.' For some time he refused. But finally he said to himself, 'Even though I don't fear God or care about men, yet because this widow keeps bothering me, I will see that she gets justice, so that she won't eventually wear me out with her coming!' And the Lord said, 'Listen to what the unjust judge says. And will not God bring about justice for his chosen ones, who cry out to him day and night? Will he keep putting them off? I tell you, he will see that they get justice, and quickly.*

How long can we wear another person's shoes? In other words, how long can we pray for someone else, longing in our hearts for them. Intercession is about persistently considering the needs and struggles of others with the compassionate heart of Christ.

c. **"Leave us alone!"**

Remember that we are in a war and we are not fighting men and women, but spiritual beings. How does persistence and authority play into this battle? Look at this verse in Mark, and notice how the demonic responded to Jesus:

Mark 1:23-24 (NKJV) *Now there was a man in their synagogue with an unclean spirit. And he cried out, saying, "Let us alone! What have we to do with You, Jesus of Nazareth? Did You come to destroy us? I know who You are—the Holy One of God!"*

Notice the response of the demonic to Jesus was basically, "Leave us alone!" When we start to move in true intercession to tear down strongholds and to free people from bondage, we get the same response. When we move in persistence, we not only "bother" the demonic, we take back all they have stolen!

....

DANIEL'S AND NEHEMIAH'S INTERCESSION

Daniel and Nehemiah are excellent examples of intercession in the Scripture:

Daniel was overwhelmed with the situation in Jerusalem. His people had been in exile for 70 years; Jerusalem had been destroyed; all his countrymen were carried away as prisoners; his heart was broken over the devastation of God's city. He knew the exile was not random, but judgment from the Lord due to the sin of his people.

In his great prayer in Daniel 9, he identified with the sins of his people and called them his own. He interceded for them. This prayer did not cause his people to be forgiven individually, for each person is accountable for their own sin. However, he was interceding and pleading with God for mercy. He asked God to forgive them as a group so blessing could again be released to the people of Israel for the rebuilding of Jerusalem.

Daniel knew the Messiah would come from Israel. But without Israel being a nation, how could the Messiah come? So Daniel "stood in the gap" where no one else would—in prayer.

Examine Daniel's prayer to understand the language of an intercessor who is repenting on behalf of his people. There are four things that mark this type of prayer:

1. **Faith.**
   Confessing generational sin is an act of faith! We have to believe that God can conquer the stronghold and bring healing. We must believe that God is able to turn everything around, no matter how far things have gone! We confess in faith that our generations have functioned in ways that are deeply sinful, and we ask God for mercy and forgiveness so that a new day can begin.

2. **Identification.**
   When we confess generational sin we must come humbly, with contrite hearts, because in reality we are not above the sin we confess. With a heart of humble identification we must acknowledge our capacity to sin and be willing to confess for those who have gone before us. People often do not want to confess sins that they have not personally committed (or even see themselves capable of committing). The broken and humble intercessors see their heart as sinful and capable of anything. In this way, repenting on behalf of a nation, city, church, or family is easy.

3. **Acknowledge the reality of our enemy.**
   Intercessors understand that the enemy is real. Paul wrote in Ephesians 6 that we battle against spiritual darkness, not people. This is not fiction. Intercessors are desperate to see all the enemy's strongholds torn down!

4. **Perceive the shadow.**
   A generational shadow is a pattern of sin that runs through many generations. To "perceive a shadow" is to look at your own life and see evidence of sin passed down as part of your family history.

   Example:
   If bitterness is a part of your parent's life, there is probably a hint of it in your own life. So shadows of the past continue to play out in the present-day. A Daniel-like intercessor proactively seeks out any shadow that could hinder him and repents.

   Look at the prayer of Daniel on the next page. For a prayer with a similar heart turn to Nehemiah 1:6.

Daniel 9 (NIV) . . . *in the first year of his reign, I, Daniel, understood from the Scriptures, according to the word of the LORD given to Jeremiah the prophet, that the desolation of Jerusalem would last seventy years. So I turned to the LORD God and pleaded with him in prayer and petition, in fasting, and in sackcloth and ashes. I prayed to the LORD my God and confessed: "O LORD, the great and awesome God, who keeps his covenant of love with all who love him and obey his commands,* **we have sinned and done wrong. We have been wicked and have rebelled; we have turned away from your commands and laws**. *We have not listened to your servants the prophets, who spoke in your name to our kings, our princes and our fathers, and to all the people of the land.*

"LORD, you are righteous, but this day we are covered with shame—the men of Judah and people of Jerusalem and all Israel, both near and far, in all the countries where you have scattered us because of our unfaithfulness to you. **O LORD, we and our kings, our princes and our fathers are covered with shame because we have sinned against you**. *The LORD our God is merciful and forgiving, even though we have rebelled against him; we have not obeyed the LORD our God or kept the laws he gave us through his servants the prophets. All Israel has transgressed your law and turned away, refusing to obey you.*

"Therefore the curses and sworn judgments written in the Law of Moses, the servant of God, have been poured out on us, because we have sinned against you. You have fulfilled the words spoken against us and against our rulers by bringing upon us great disaster. Under the whole heaven nothing has ever been done like what has been done to Jerusalem. Just as it is written in the Law of Moses, all this disaster has come upon us, yet we have not sought the favor of the LORD our God by turning from our sins and giving attention to your truth. The LORD did not hesitate to bring the disaster upon us, for the LORD our God is righteous in everything he does; yet we have not obeyed him.

"Now, O LORD our God, who brought your people out of Egypt with a mighty hand and who made for yourself a name that endures to this day, we have sinned, we have done wrong. O LORD, in keeping with all your righteous acts, turn away your anger and your wrath from Jerusalem, your city, your holy hill. **Our sins and the iniquities of our fathers have made Jerusalem and your people an object of scorn to all those around us**.

"Now, our God, hear the prayers and petitions of your servant. For your sake, O LORD, look with favor on your desolate sanctuary. Give ear, O God, and hear; open your eyes and see the desolation of the city that bears your Name. We do not make requests of you because we are righteous, but because of your great mercy. **O LORD, listen! O LORD, forgive!** *O LORD, hear and act! For your sake, O my God, do not delay, because your city and your people bear your Name."*

Note: It is interesting to note that Daniel owned the sin of Israel and the previous generations of Israel that had led to their severe judgment. Yet, in Daniel 6:4, we are told that Daniel's contemporaries tried to find accusations against Daniel that would disqualify him—but they could not. It was a godly man who entered into a prayer of confession with deep conviction and ownership because he understood the reality of the "corporate one" (the community) and the consequences of sin in generations past.

THE INFLUENCE OF THE GENERATIONS

The Scriptures repeatedly speak to the inter-relationship and influence that previous generations have on current ones. Western Culture does not readily recognize and understand this truth; but there are generational patterns that you can probably identify in your family.

Exodus 34:7 (NLT) *I show this unfailing love to many thousands by forgiving every kind of sin and rebellion. Even so I do not leave sin unpunished, but I punish the children for the sins of their parents to the third and fourth generations.*

Psalm 112:1-2 (NLT) *Praise the LORD! Happy are those who fear the LORD. Yes, happy are those who delight in doing what he commands. Their children will be successful everywhere; an entire generation of godly people will be blessed.*

The great news is that we can stop the destructive generational patterns of sinful strongholds while initiating and reinforcing generational patterns of blessings. The Scriptures tell us how this can be done, and give us examples of this taking place.

Leviticus 26:40, 42 (NASB) *If they confess their iniquity and the iniquity of their forefathers, in their unfaithfulness which they committed against Me, and also in their acting with hostility against Me . . . then I will remember My covenant with Jacob, and I will remember also My covenant with Isaac, and My covenant with Abraham as well, and I will remember the land.*

This is what Daniel was being faithful to in his prayer in Daniel 9. As a result, Judah, which was in exile as judgment, was freed. Nehemiah prayed in the exact same pattern in Nehemiah 1 and 9. As a result, a ruined Jerusalem was supernaturally restored.

BIBLICAL EXAMPLES OF GENERATIONAL PATTERNS

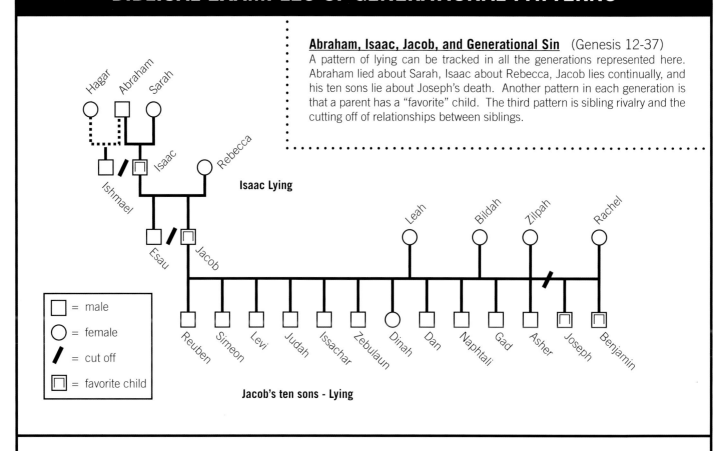

Abraham, Isaac, Jacob, and Generational Sin (Genesis 12-37)
A pattern of lying can be tracked in all the generations represented here. Abraham lied about Sarah, Isaac about Rebecca, Jacob lies continually, and his ten sons lie about Joseph's death. Another pattern in each generation is that a parent has a "favorite" child. The third pattern is sibling rivalry and the cutting off of relationships between siblings.

Isaac Lying

Jacob's ten sons - Lying

□ = male
○ = female
／ = cut off
▣ = favorite child

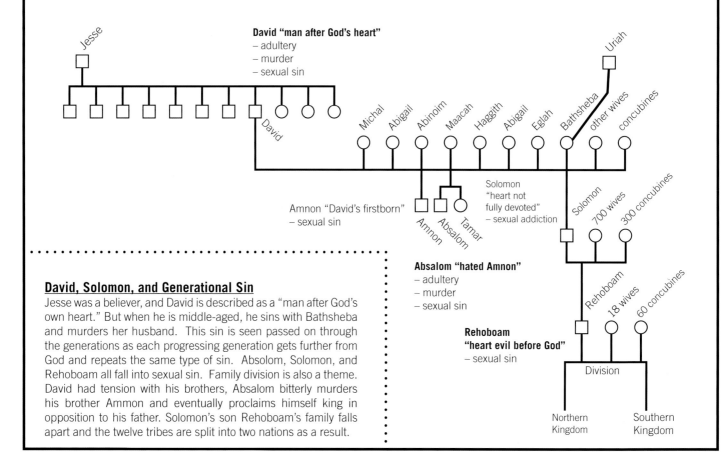

David "man after God's heart"
– adultery
– murder
– sexual sin

Amnon "David's firstborn"
– sexual sin

Solomon
"heart not fully devoted"
– sexual addiction

Absalom "hated Amnon"
– adultery
– murder
– sexual sin

Rehoboam
"heart evil before God"
– sexual sin

Division

Northern Kingdom   Southern Kingdom

David, Solomon, and Generational Sin
Jesse was a believer, and David is described as a "man after God's own heart." But when he is middle-aged, he sins with Bathsheba and murders her husband. This sin is seen passed on through the generations as each progressing generation gets further from God and repeats the same type of sin. Absolom, Solomon, and Rehoboam all fall into sexual sin. Family division is also a theme. David had tension with his brothers, Absalom bitterly murders his brother Ammon and eventually proclaims himself king in opposition to his father. Solomon's son Rehoboam's family falls apart and the twelve tribes are split into two nations as a result.

GENERATIONAL PATTERNS CHECKLIST

Pray like Daniel for breakthrough in your own life and family! Go through the checkboxes below. They highlight some sin areas that might run through your generations. The Lord might bring to mind specific patterns that have existed in your family for generations. *This list is not comprehensive, so take the time to seek the Lord yourself for patterns.*

The key in this exercise is to have a heart cry of repentance. Be desperate for freedom! Be desperate not only for you, but for your children and their children. You can start a pattern of blessing today! This **cannot be just words** you speak out—it must be **from your heart**. There is sin that has marked your family for years. In desperation and a broken heart you can practice powerful intercession that will break every hold.

Note: In corporate prayer times, people will confess things that others cannot relate to: Maybe your family never used drugs, never used alcohol, or was never part of a false religion. This is all okay because it is all about intercession. You are becoming a Daniel and praying on behalf of yourself and everyone in the room. You are crying out for strongholds and chains to be broken over families! Pray with great faith, believing that every word of your prayer will be answered.

1. **Passivity.**
   - ❑ Withholding words of blessings—parent to child.
   - ❑ Withholding affection—parent to child.
   - ❑ Lack of discipline from parents (which caused turmoil both physically and spiritually because discipline was not done right).
   - ❑ Pattern of backsliding into sin.
   - ❑ Hesitation in obedience to God or other authority.

2. **Temporal Values.**
   - ❑ Love of money and possessions.
   - ❑ More concerned with physical comfort than godly obedience.
   - ❑ Parents more concerned with self and positions or possessions than children.
   - ❑ Children not honored, seen as a burden.
   - ❑ Little concern for God's truth.

3. **Anger.**
   - ❑ Verbal abuse.
   - ❑ Physical abuse.
   - ❑ Fits of rage.
   - ❑ Biting sarcasm, tearing down.
   - ❑ Withdrawal because of inverted anger.
   - ❑ Blaming, fault finding, criticalness.

4. **Unbelief.**
   - ❑ A general distrust in God which leads to distrust in authority.
   - ❑ Ignoring God completely or saying, "God is far away," or "Where was God when . . ."
   - ❑ Daily anxiety.
   - ❑ Fear of not being provided for (not having enough to pay the bills, etc.)
   - ❑ Love of knowledge; dependence on human reason and ingenuity vs. the truth of God.

5. **Insignificance.**
   - ❑ Loneliness, despair, sorrow, and depression.
   - ❑ Patterns of abandonment.
   - ❑ Suicide.
   - ❑ Self-hatred; self-deprecation.
   - ❑ Anorexia, control, manipulation, and destruction of your own body.

6. **Rebellion.**
   - ❑ Overt disregard of conscience and/or knowledge of Christ.
   - ❑ Divorce, critical heart, blame.
   - ❑ Adultery.
   - ❑ Any sexual immorality.
   - ❑ Drug addiction.
   - ❑ Alcoholism.
   - ❑ Occult involvement (including false religions).
   - ❑ Murder (not just the physical act, but a heart of hatred).

SAMPLE PRAYER TO BREAK GENERATIONAL PATTERNS:

REPENT	Lord Jesus, please forgive me for the sin of _____. I know it is not only my sin, but has been a part of my family for generations. We have sinned against you in this way. I turn from this sin right now! Set me free from this bondage! Oh Lord, I plead for freedom and release from this pattern of sin that has been a part of my generations!
RECEIVE	Lord Jesus, I receive your forgiveness for this sin. Thank you for releasing me from this sin that has marked my family line for generations! I ask that you empower me with your Holy Spirit to walk out full repentance as I replace the old lies with Your truth!
REBUKE	Right now, in the full authority of Jesus Christ, I sever every tie to this sin that has come through the generations before me! I command you to flee, right now, enemy! You are a liar, you will no longer hold me, nor my family captive. We will no longer be marked by this sin! You can't have me! You can't have my children! I sever every curse associated with this sin!
REPLACE	Lord Jesus, I declare that I am walking in the opposite direction of this sin. I choose with all my heart and mind to run after You in obedience and truth! **2 Chronicles 7:14 (NIV)** . . . if my people, who are called by my name, will humble themselves and pray and seek my face and turn from their wicked ways, then will I hear from heaven and will forgive their sin and will heal their land.

(ENDNOTES)

1. Webster's New Twentieth Century Dictionary Of the English Language, ed. Jean L. McKechnie, (William Collins and World Publishing Company; 1977).
2. Peter Scazzero. *The Emotionally Healthy Church* (Grand Rapids: Zondervan, 2003), 91, 94. Graphics of Generational Patterns on page 48 where used with permission from this highly recommended resource.

APPLICATION

Closing Questions

1. Answer the question, "What does it means to intercede?" in your own words.

2. How did (does) Jesus interceed for us?

3. What does it mean to "identify" with the sin in your prior generations? How did Daniel do this in his prayer in Daniel 9?

4. What generational patterns can you easily recognize in your own family? Are there patterns that have become so normal you expect them to continue?

Group Prayer Declaration

Tear down these patterns! It is wonderful to know that through the power of Christ you and your family do not have to continue to be robbed of joy and intimacy in Christ. Your teacher will lead you in praying to break these patterns (look at the sample prayer on the last page). If you would like to continue at home, you are encouraged to do so. Why not be as thorough as possible? We do not want to repeat the same sin patterns as the generations before us!

Homework

Take a look at the Resource Section at the end of the book. In it you will find some helpful articles.

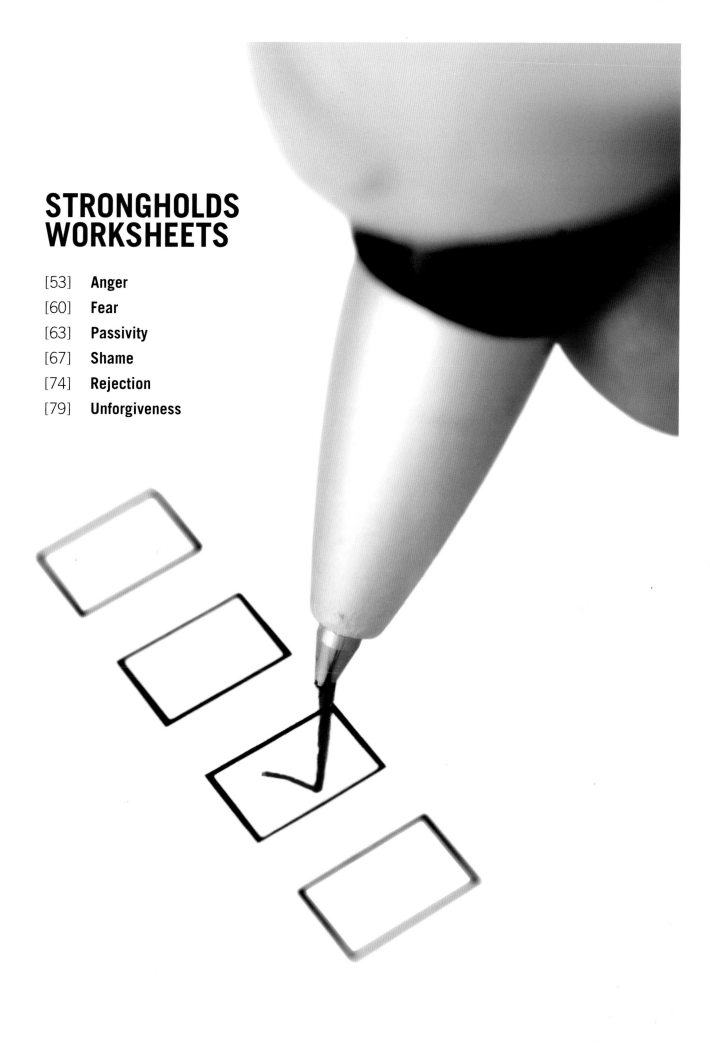

STRONGHOLDS
WORKSHEETS

[53]   **Anger**

[60]   **Fear**

[63]   **Passivity**

[67]   **Shame**

[74]   **Rejection**

[79]   **Unforgiveness**

ANGER

INTRODUCTION

Ecclesiastes 7:8-10 (NASB) *The end of a thing is better than its beginning; the patient in spirit is better than the proud in spirit. Do not hasten in your spirit to be angry, for anger rests in the bosom of fools. Do not say, "Why were the former days better than these?" For you do not inquire wisely concerning this.*

The Bible tells us that "anger rests in the bosom of fools." Beneath anger lies bitterness, and unresolved bitterness creates resentment, anger, and deep emotional and spiritual damage. Paul traced the development of unresolved bitterness in Ephesians 4:31: Bitterness leads to wrath (outbursts of anger), wrath leads to anger (rage; a constant state of anger), anger leads to clamor (making a public scene), clamor is followed by slander (false charges or misrepresentations), and slander leads to malice (inner hatred of the heart). The danger of harboring an attitude of bitterness is that, eventually, it will control you.

Paul warns that bitterness is like a root. The longer it grows, the more difficult it is to dig out. Hebrews 12:15 states that a root of bitterness left to grow brings defilement "to the many." The root will produce the fruit of anger, ungratefulness, a critical attitude, insensitivity toward others, revenge, mistrust, and depression. Unresolved bitterness is like a highly contagious disease that contaminates and destroys us and others.

The cure for bitterness and anger is forgiveness. In order to resolve bitterness, we must first understand and experience God's forgiveness of our sin. God chose to focus on His desire to forgive us rather than to hold us accountable for our failures (Isaiah 43:25, 55:7; Psalm 103:12). Forgiveness demands a payment. When someone sins against us and hurts us, our sense of justice demands that a fair payment be made to us for their failure. If that person cannot pay (or chooses not to pay), we either resent the injustice and become bitter and angry, or we exercise forgiveness that leads to peace. Forgiveness is not easy, especially when something has caused great harm. However, as we free the offender through forgiveness, we free ourselves from the effects of destructive attitudes.

The worksheet that follows is designed to help identify areas of unforgiveness, bitterness, or anger that need to be resolved. *Keep in mind that one indicator for whether or not true forgiveness has occurred is the ability (through the Holy Spirit) to pray a powerful blessing on the person who hurt us.*

SOME SYMPTOMS OF ANGER

❑ I feel relatively happy, and then I am struck with a sudden mood change.

❑ I raise my voice (and even yell) to communicate something that I am emphatic about.

❑ I have an expressed impatience with others that often plays out in exasperation. "Why can't they understand?"

❑ I often anticipate another person's predictable behavior, and I become angry when I see it fulfilled.

❑ I become angry when others "cannot read my mind." I want others to think just like I think, and to anticipate what I need.

❑ I become angry when I am not recognized for my contribution.

❑ I become angry when I feel that I am disrespected, or when my words are not taken seriously.

❑ I know I am angry because of the language inside my head (cursing of myself or others).

❑ I know I am angry when I do not want to hear what another person has to say.

❑ I get angry when others do not make me a priority.

❑ I get angry when I do not have what I need.

❑ I get angry when people do not do what I say.

❑ I get angry when I cannot control a given situation.

❑ I get angry about suggestions that I have done something wrong.

❑ I get angry when I feel added pressure at work, with finances, with personal responsibilities, and/or my or others' expectations.

❑ I easily become defensive about myself and about others.

❑ I quickly see faults in others.

❑ I look for opportunities to bring up old, hurtful subjects.

❑ I speak negatively or critically of others.

❑ The phrase "I don't deserve this" goes through my head frequently.

❑ I say I have forgiven, but I continue to reprocess those subjects in my mind.

❑ I get frustrated about the perceived faults and mistakes of others.

❑ I become impatient easily.

❑ I think my life is harder than others. "I have been given a raw deal."

BIOLOGICAL FATHER/STEPFATHER

Check all boxes that apply and add your own thoughts as needed. This will help you to discover how to extend forgiveness to your father/stepfather.

Were the following elements present in your relationship?

❑ **Exasperation:** Overuse of, or a faulty form of, discipline that left you crushed in spirit or confused about what you did wrong.

❑ **Control/Manipulation:** Did he use guilt to get you to obey him? Did he emotionally manipulate you?

❑ **Absence of spiritual leadership:** Did your father stand watch over the spiritual condition of the home?

❑ **Neglect:** Did your father spend time with you on a consistent basis?

❑ **Abandonment:** Were you left in front of the TV or left in the care of people other than your parents on a consistent basis?

❑ **Rejection:** Did your parents want you as a child? Were you accepted by your father?

❑ **Passivity:** Did your father lead the home? Did your father initiate? Did he allow your mother to do what the Lord expected of her?

❑ **Criticism:** Was your father critical of you, your abilities, interests, etc.?

❑ **Performance-based acceptance and love:** Were you rewarded with words of encouragement only when you measured up to what your father expected of you?

❑ **Alcohol abuse.**

❑ **Drug use.**

❑ **Pornography.**

❑ **Adultery.**

❑ **Divorce.**

❑ **Physical abuse.**

❑ **Emotional abuse.**

❑ **Sexual abuse.**

The following sins of omission are things that your father did not do. Often these sins are more damaging than sins of commission:

❑ **Withheld affection**

❑ **Withheld blessing**

❑ **Withheld words of encouragement**

❑ **Withheld discipline**

These areas may lead to a great deal of hurt and bitterness:

❑ **Were your brothers or sisters treated in a way that left you bitter?**

❑ **Was your mother treated by your father in a way that left you bitter?**

The items checked on the preceding list must be brought to the cross. A sample prayer is provided below to help guide you through the process. James 5:16 states that as you confess your sin to one another you will be healed. It is essential to have a witness supporting you as you walk through these prayers.

LORD JESUS, I FORGIVE MY FATHER (STEPFATHER) for the sin of _____. *(say here all of the sins for which you need to forgive your father and go through it all at one time.)* Lord Jesus, I ask you to forgive me for the sin of unforgiveness toward my father for these sins. Forgive me for bitterness, resentment, and anger toward him. I ask your forgiveness for rebellion against my father, and I now break all curses, negative thoughts, and slander I have spoken against him. I replace those curses now with mighty blessings!

JESUS, I NOW WANT TO PRAY A BLESSING ON MY FATHER. *(Stand up to pray. Pray forcefully, with all of your heart and strength; raise your voice if you need to and pray with faith.)*

I pray that you will:
- ❑ bless him with salvation.
- ❑ bless him with the same freedom I have found today.
- ❑ bless him with a new and soft heart.
- ❑ bless his marriage.
- ❑ bless his finances and his work.
- ❑ bless him with joy, peace, kindness, love, and all of the fruit of the Spirit (Galatians 5:22).
- ❑ bless him with freedom from condemnation and shame. Heal his wounds.
- ❑ bless him with a long life and with great health.
- ❑ bless him with freedom from all of the schemes and plans of Satan.
  - ☑ I declare that I love my father.
  - ☑ I declare that my father is your child.
  - ☑ I look at him through your eyes, and see his hurt and his pain.
  - ☑ I ask in faith that you would pour your Spirit on him. Do it now, Lord! My chains are broken and I stand free before you. Thank you for the power of the cross.

REBUKE

*Stand up and pray the following prayer with conviction, with all of your heart, and with faith that God will move in a powerful way right **now**. Pray until you and your group leader sense a release.*

JESUS, I RENOUNCE a life of anger, bitterness, and unforgiveness. I renounce the right to take offense. I give up my right to see justice. I give you my relationship with my father; it is in your hands now. I am not responsible for things that only you can do. I cut that cord now! I rebuke the spirits of:

☑	Rejection	☑	Abandonment
☑	Anger	☑	Bitterness
☑	Unforgiveness	☑	Division
☑	Sickness	☑	Control

REPLACE

When thoughts of bitterness occur again, rebuke them and stand firm on not taking offense again. If possible, write a short letter to tell your father you love him, and write an honest blessing toward him. Do not criticize him in this letter; simply bless him and let the results rest in the Lord's hands.

BIOLOGICAL MOM/STEPMOM

Check all boxes that apply and add your own thoughts as needed. This will help you to discover how to extend forgiveness to your mother/stepmother.

Were the following elements present in your relationship?

- ❑ **Exasperation:** Overuse of or a faulty form of discipline that left you crushed in spirit or confused about what you did wrong.
- ❑ **Control/Manipulation.** Did she use guilt to get you to obey her? Did she emotionally manipulate you?
- ❑ **Absence of spiritual leadership:** Did your mother stand watch over the spiritual condition of the home?
- ❑ **Neglect:** Did your mother spend time with you on a consistent basis?
- ❑ **Abandonment:** Were you left in front of the TV or left in the care of people other than your parents on a consistent basis?
- ❑ **Rejection:** Did your parents want you as a child? Were you accepted by your mother?
- ❑ **Passivity:** Did your mother lead the home? Did your mother initiate? Did she allow your father to do what the Lord expected of him?
- ❑ **Criticism:** Was your mother critical of you, your abilities, your interests, etc.?

- ❏ **Performance-based acceptance and love:** Were you rewarded with words of encouragement only when you measured up to what your mother expected of you?
- ❏ **Alcohol abuse.**
- ❏ **Drug use.**
- ❏ **Pornography.**
- ❏ **Adultery.**
- ❏ **Divorce.**
- ❏ **Physical abuse.**
- ❏ **Emotional abuse.**
- ❏ **Sexual abuse.**

The following sins of omission are things that your mother did not do. Often these sins are more damaging than sins of commission:

- ❏ **Withheld affection.**
- ❏ **Withheld blessing.**
- ❏ **Withheld words of encouragement.**
- ❏ **Withheld discipline.**

These areas may lead to a great deal of hurt and bitterness:

- ❏ **Were your brothers or sisters treated in a way that left you bitter?**
- ❏ **Was your father treated by your mother in a way that left you bitter?**

The items checked on the preceding list must be brought to the cross. A sample prayer is provided below to help guide you through the process. James 5:16 states that as you confess your sins to one another you will be healed. It is essential to have a witness who supports you as you walk through these prayers.

LORD JESUS, I FORGIVE MY MOTHER (STEP-MOTHER) for the sin of _____ . *(say here all of the sins for which you need to forgive your mother and go through it all at one time.)* Lord Jesus, I ask you to forgive me for the sin of unforgiveness toward my mother because of these sins. Forgive me for bitterness, resentment, and anger toward my mother. I ask your forgiveness for rebellion against my mother, and I now break all curses, negative thoughts, or slander I have spoken against her. I replace those curses now with mighty blessings!

JESUS, I NOW PRAY A BLESSING ON MY MOTHER. *(Stand up to pray. Pray forcefully, with all of your heart and strength; raise your voice if need be and pray with faith.)*

I pray that you will:
- ❏ bless her with salvation.
- ❏ bless her with the same freedom I have found today.
- ❏ bless her with a new and soft heart.
- ❏ bless her marriage.
- ❏ bless her finances and his work.
- ❏ bless her with joy, peace, kindness, love, and all of the fruit of the Spirit (Galatians 5:22).
- ❏ bless her with freedom from condemnation and shame. Heal her wounds.
- ❏ bless her with a long life and with great health.
- ❏ bless her with freedom from all of the schemes and plans of Satan.
  - ☑ I declare that I love my mother.
  - ☑ I declare that my mother is your child.
  - ☑ I look at her through your eyes, and see her hurt and her pain.
  - ☑ I ask in faith that you would pour your Spirit on her. Do it now, Lord! My chains are broken and I stand free before you. Thank you for the power of the cross.

REBUKE

*Stand up and pray the following prayer with conviction, with all of your heart, and with faith that God will move in a powerful way right **now**. Pray until you and your group leader sense a release.*

JESUS, I RENOUNCE a life of anger, bitterness, and unforgiveness. I renounce the right to take offense. I give up my right to see justice. I give you my relationship with my mother; it is in your hands now. I am not responsible for things that only you can do. I cut that cord now! I rebuke the spirits of:

☑ Rejection	☑ Abandonment
☑ Anger	☑ Bitterness
☑ Unforgiveness	☑ Division
☑ Sickness	☑ Control

REPLACE

When thoughts of bitterness occur again, rebuke them and stand firm on not taking offense again. If possible, write a short letter to tell your mother you love her, and write an honest blessing toward her. Do not criticize her in this letter; simply bless her and let the results rest in the Lord's hands.

SIBLINGS AND FRIENDS

Look for areas in which you may not have forgiven people:

❑ **Rejection:** Write down names here, as we need to be specific.

_____

_____

❑ **Jealousy.**
❑ **Competition.**
❑ **Betrayal.**

LORD JESUS, I ASK YOU TO FORGIVE ME for all unforgiveness, anger, and bitterness that I have held toward _____. I forgive them for rejection, betrayal, and _____ *(any other specific instances that come to mind)*. I break all curses that I have spoken against them, and I replace those now with great blessings. I no longer take offense; I am free of all bitterness and anger. I bless them! *(Declare at least ten different blessings)*.

GIRLFRIENDS AND BOYFRIENDS

❑ **Rejection.**
❑ **Betrayal.**

WHAT IS A SOUL TIE?

Soul ties are formed when relationships depart from Biblical guidelines in one or more areas, resulting in an unhealthy connection between people. The relationship has stepped outside of the truth of God's Word. In many cases, the sin of "fear of man" enters these relationships. The result is confusion.

For example, you may try to convince a person that a relationship is damaging and causes the rest of the family to suffer from the consequences of that damage. Examples to consider are many, but a few are included below:

1. Unhealthy and codependent relationships with family members. The following thoughts plague you: "What would happen if I did not call every day to check in?" "What would happen if I actually confronted the person with truth?"
2. Involvement with friendships that cause you to stumble on a consistent basis with various sins, but you are afraid to truly speak your convictions because you fear rejection.
3. You receive council from several people regarding a relationship that has an adverse effect on you, but you are not able to see it yourself. An example could be a married woman's relationship with her mother. Where decisions are made based primarily on what her mother believes versus the married woman's husband. "We have to go over there or my mom will be so upset." "If we do not go on vacation with them they will be devastated." "We had better send a gift or a card or we will never hear the end of it."

4. You struggle with the ability to confront someone in a godly manner. For example, the Lord asks you to confront a person with God's truth, but out of fear you avoid it and will not speak the truth.
5. Avoidance of speaking the truth is a key symptom of a soul tie.

The term soul tie has to do with a sinful priority system in which the enemy is entrenched. Remember the simplicity of following Jesus: Hear and obey what the Scriptures teach immediately. Do so with joy, and a thankful heart. With issues of spiritual health, the first thought in your mind is, "What would Jesus have me do?" and not, "What will this other person think if I obey the Lord?" If the latter is true, fear of people takes the place of the fear of God.

Proverbs 9:10 (NIV) *The fear of the LORD is the beginning of wisdom.*

Psalm 118:6 (NKJV) *The LORD is on my side; I will not fear. What can man do to me?"*

When you function in the fear of people versus the Lord, you will always live in deception.

A soul tie can be formed as a result of physical intimacy outside of marriage, which is a false union between two people. Along with the sin of premarital sex that needs to be confessed, soul ties need to be severed through the power of the blood of Jesus. Because a sexual union outside of marriage is not created in godly love, it leaves residual hatred toward the other person. God says that our love for another is to be pure, but that cannot be secured outside of the covering of the marriage relationship. Hatred born out of this violation can also turn into self-hatred, rejection, and distrust of others.

Common attributes of a soul tie are:

1. Seeking the approval of another person above God's approval. This prevents us from obeying God, because we may be fearful of what someone will think.
2. Living in another person's mind; desiring approval, attention, or recognition from that person.
3. Living in a state of confusion with regard to another person. You may be unable to make a simple decision of obedience because of the weight given to the opinions of another person.
4. You care more about what another person thinks than what the Lord thinks.

Sample prayer for a soul tie that is <u>not part of sexual sin</u>:

Lord Jesus, I ask you to forgive me for the sin of fear of man in regard to my relationship with _____. I have placed this relationship as a greater priority than obedience to you. I lived making decisions based on what they think versus what the Scripture teaches. Forgive me for indecision, confusion, and all rebellion.

I rebuke in Jesus' name all confusion, fear, rebellion, resistance ("I don't want to deal with it."), and all anger or passivity related to this soul tie.

Sample prayer for a soul tie that formed <u>because of sexual sin</u>:

Lord Jesus, I ask you to forgive me for the sin of sex outside of marriage. I ask forgiveness for rebellion and the disregard that was shown towards this other person. I walk away from these sins, and through the powerful name of Jesus Christ, I break the union that was forged between me and _____. I command everything that came in through these sins to go to the feet of Jesus: Hatred, self-hatred, rejection, rebellion, anger and fear must go to the feet of Jesus. (Remember that you need to move in God's authority and power as you rebuke the enemy.)

COACHES AND TEACHERS

❑ _____

❑ _____

❑ _____

❑ _____

ANYONE ELSE THE SPIRIT BRINGS TO MIND

❑ _____

❑ _____

❑ _____

❑ _____

Are there any other specific instances the Lord brings to your mind?

_____

_____

_____

_____

_____

SAMPLE PRAYER

Lord Jesus, I forgive _____ for the sin or rejection and betrayal (or other things that come to mind). I ask your forgiveness now for how I treated them (confess whatever sins the Lord brings to your attention). I ask your forgiveness now for all unforgiveness I held toward them, and for all anger and resentment. I cut all soul ties by the blood of Jesus. By the blood of Jesus Christ I break all words that cursed instead of blessed, and I now bless them with:

❑ Salvation.

❑ Filling of your Holy Spirit.

❑ Unconditional love in a rich marriage and family life.

❑ Complete freedom.

❑ Healthy friendships.

❑ Financial provision.

❑ A wonderful church to attend.

REBUKE

Jesus, I now renounce a life of anger, bitterness, and unforgiveness. I renounce the right to take offense. I give up my right to see justice. I give you these relationships, and they are in your hands now. I am not responsible for things only you can do. I cut that cord now. Satan, I rebuke you and all of your spirits of:

☑ Rejection	☑ Abandonment
☑ Anger	☑ Bitterness
☑ Unforgiveness	☑ Division
☑ Sickness	☑ Control

As you work through the following section, do not limit yourself only to what is on this page. There may be other incidents or items that need to be taken to the cross. As you go through this, it will be extremely helpful for you to mark the boxes next to things for which you need to forgive your husband/ wife, and things for which you need to ask his/her forgiveness.

SPOUSE/EX SPOUSE

Are the following elements present in your relationship or in past relationships? These are sins of commission (committed against another person):

- ❑ Unfaithfulness or betrayal.
- ❑ Control/Manipulation.
- ❑ Absence of spiritual leadership: Did your husband stand watch over the spiritual condition of the home?
- ❑ Neglect.
- ❑ Abandonment.
- ❑ Rejection.
- ❑ Passivity.
- ❑ Criticism.
- ❑ Performance-based acceptance and love.
- ❑ Lies.
- ❑ Alcohol abuse.
- ❑ Drug use.
- ❑ Pornography.
- ❑ Adultery.
- ❑ Divorce.
- ❑ Physical abuse.
- ❑ Emotional abuse.
- ❑ Sexual abuse.

The following sins of omission are things that your husband or wife did not do. Often these sins are more damaging than sins of commission:

- ❑ **Withholding affection.**
- ❑ **Withholding blessing.**
- ❑ **Withholding words of encouragement.**

The items checked on the list above need to be brought to the cross. A sample prayer is provided to help guide you through the process. Remember, James 5:16 tells us that as we confess our sins to one another we will be healed. It is essential that you have a witness to support you as you walk through these prayers.

LORD JESUS, I FORGIVE MY HUSBAND/WIFE for the sin of
_____. (List here all of the sins for which you need to forgive your husband/wife, and pray through each one separately). Lord Jesus, I ask you to forgive me for the sin of unforgiveness toward my husband/

wife for these sins. Forgive me for bitterness, resentment, and anger toward my husband/wife. I ask your forgiveness for rebellion toward my husband/wife, and I now break all curses, negative thoughts, or slander I have spoken against him/her. I replace those curses now with mighty blessings!

JESUS, I WANT TO PRAY A BLESSING ON MY HUSBAND/WIFE
(Stand up to pray this prayer. Pray forcefully, with all of your heart and strength; raise your voice if you need to and pray with faith). Jesus, I pray that you will:

- ❑ Bless him/her with salvation.
- ❑ Bless him/her with the same freedom I found today.
- ❑ Bless him/her with a new and soft heart.
- ❑ Bless his/her marriage.
- ❑ Bless his/her finances and work.
- ❑ Bless him/her with joy, peace, kindness, love, and all of the fruit of the Spirit.
- ❑ Bless him/her so that he/she will be free of condemnation and shame. Heal his/her wounds.
- ❑ Bless him/her with a long life and great health.
- ❑ Bless him/her with freedom from all of the schemes and plans of Satan.
    - ☑ I declare that I love my husband/wife.
    - ☑ I declare that my husband/wife is your child.
    - ☑ I look at him/her through your eyes, and see his/her hurt and pain.
    - ☑ I ask in faith that you pour your fire on him/her. Do it now, Lord!

REBUKE

Stand up and pray the following prayer with conviction, with all of your heart, and with faith that God will move in a powerful way right **now**. Pray until you and your group leader sense a release.

Jesus, I now renounce a life of anger, bitterness, and unforgiveness. I renounce the right to take offense. I give up my right to see justice. I give you this relationship with my husband/wife, and it is in your hands now. I am not responsible for things that only you can do. I cut that cord now! I rebuke the spirits of:

☑	Rejection	☑	Abandonment
☑	Anger	☑	Bitterness
☑	Unforgiveness	☑	Division
☑	Sickness	☑	Control

MY CHAINS ARE BROKEN AND I STAND FREE BEFORE YOU. THANK YOU LORD FOR THE POWER OF THE CROSS!

FEAR

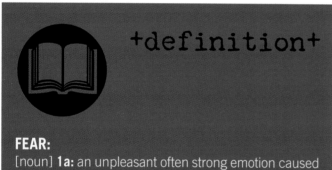

+definition+

FEAR:
[noun] **1a:** an unpleasant often strong emotion caused by anticipation or awareness of danger **1b:** (1): an instance of this emotion (2): a state marked by this emotion.

DECEIVE:
[verb] **synonyms** *MISLEAD, DELUDE, BEGUILE mean to lead astray or frustrate usually by underhandedness. DECEIVE implies imposing a false idea or belief that causes ignorance, bewilderment, or helplessness.* [1]

Most of us do not realize how deeply fear is rooted in our every day life. The nature of fear is to *deceive*. The Scriptures make it very clear that the Lord wants us to be free from fear. Freedom from fear is gained as we:

1. **Allow the power of the Holy Spirit to uncover the presence of fear in our lives.**

2. **Bring fears to the cross through repentance and affirming God's truth.**

3. **Commit to take action to move in the opposite spirit.**

WHERE DOES FEAR COME FROM?

1. **It is not from God.**

   2 Timothy 1:7 (NIV) *For God did not give us a spirit of timidity, but a spirit of power, of love and of self-discipline.*

2. **It is a result of a lack of faith.**

   Matthew 14:30-31 (NIV) *But when he saw the wind, he was afraid and beginning to sink, cried out, "Lord save me!" Immediately Jesus reached out his hand and caught him. "You of little faith," he said. "Why did you doubt?"*

EXAMPLES OF LIVING IN FEAR

Check all the boxes that apply to you:

1. **Fear of punishment: Little peace, hope, faith, or joy.**

   1 John 4:18 (NKJV) *There is no fear in love; but perfect love casts out fear, because fear involves torment.*

   ❑ My prayer times and Bible reading are motivated by fear.
   ❑ My relationship with Jesus is performance-based.
   ❑ I fear failing God.
   ❑ I fear punishment from God.

   Forms of punishment I fear:
   ❑ Withholding of financial blessing.
   ❑ Withholding of true love and forgiveness.
   ❑ God will ask me to suffer unnaturally.
   ❑ God withholding Himself, ignoring me, not listening (as though I must earn His attention as with earthly relationships).

2. **Fear of man (insecurity).**

   Proverbs 29:25 (NIV) *Fear of man will prove to be a snare, but whoever trusts in the Lord is kept safe.*

   Isaiah 51:7 (NIV) *Hear me, you who know what is right, you people who have my law in your hearts: Do not fear the reproach of men or be terrified by their insults.*

   ❑ I fear what other people think about me.
   ❑ I fear (imagined) what others say about me.
   ❑ I fear being rejected by those close to me.
   ❑ I fear people in authority.
   ❑ I fear communicating publicly.
   ❑ I fear confrontation.
   ❑ I fear being held accountable.

3. **Fear becomes a self-fulfilling prophecy.**

   Fear of failure often plays right into the hands of the enemy. Fear can work against your faith, sometimes helping to bring about the failure you fear. How often are people instructed by God or His agents: "Do not be afraid!" You are to fear nothing.

   Judges 7:3 (NIV) *. . . announce now to the people, "Anyone who trembles with fear may turn back and leave Mount Gilead." So twenty-two thousand men left, while ten thousand remained.*

❑ I fear falling back into sin.
❑ I fear that I will not be freed from habitual sins or addictions.
❑ I fear I will never get married.
❑ I fear failing in marriage.
❑ I fear that I will get divorced.
❑ I fear intimacy and being seen for who I really am.
❑ I fear that my children will not "turn out."
❑ I fear not succeeding in a good career.
❑ I fear disappointing my parents or others I respect.

4. **Fear of your past becoming known (and the possible ramifications).**

   Isaiah 54:4 (NIV) *Do not be afraid; you will not suffer shame. Do not fear disgrace; you will not be humiliated. You will forget the shame of your youth and remember no more the reproach of your widowhood.*

   ❑ I fear suffering shame from my past.
   ❑ I fear that my past may disgrace me, or hinder or stop God's work in my life.
   ❑ I fear God's punishment for my past.
   ❑ I fear confessing a struggle with sexual sin (promiscuity, pornography, homosexuality, adultery) and what others may think if I confess that struggle.
   ❑ I fear confessing shame and guilt from having had an abortion.
   ❑ I fear that I may not be healed from scars or wounds that occurred in my past.
   ❑ I fear that I will be found out for "who I really am."

5. **Sudden unnatural fears are <u>always</u> from Satan.**

   Proverbs 3:24-25 (NIV) *. . . when you lie down, you will not be afraid; when you lie down, your sleep will be sweet. Have no fear of sudden disaster or of the ruin that overtakes the wicked.*

   ❑ Hopelessness.
   ❑ Oppressive fears.
   ❑ Fear of death.
   ❑ Fear of sickness.
   ❑ Fear of spouse, parents, or children dying.
   ❑ Fear of a lack of provision.
   ❑ Fear of losing my job.
   ❑ Fear of chaotic world events.

WHAT STEPS ARE NEEDED TO DESTROY FEAR?

1. **Decisions must be made to hate the sin of fear with holy violence.** You must understand that fear grieves God's heart, for it denies the reality of His awesome provision and protection.

2. **Confess all specific areas of sin.**

3. **Ask God to reveal any areas and root issues that are still unknown to you.**

4. **Renounce fear in the name of Jesus, and rebuke the enemy in the name of Jesus and by the blood of Jesus.** Firmly command the enemy to go, and stand in faith in the battle.

5. **You must now move "in the opposite spirit,"** in the opposite direction of your fears. It is not enough to *confess* your fears; now we must *face them aggressively*, and obey the Word of God.

SCRIPTURE TO REFLECT UPON

Jeremiah 17:8 (NIV) *He will be like a tree planted by the water that sends out its roots by the stream. It does not fear when heat comes; its leaves are always green. It has no worries in a year of drought and never fails to bear fruit.*

Psalm 27:1 (NIV) *The LORD is my light and my salvation– whom shall I fear? The LORD is the stronghold of my life–of whom shall I be afraid?*

Psalm 46:1-2 (NIV) *God is our refuge and strength, an ever-present help in trouble. Therefore we will not fear, though the earth give way and the mountains fall into the heart of the sea . . .*

Romans 8:15 (NIV) *For you did not receive a spirit that makes you a slave again to fear, but you received the Spirit of sonship. And by him we cry, "Abba, Father."*

Joshua 1:9 (NIV) *Have I not commanded you? Be strong and courageous. Do not be terrified; do not be discouraged, for the LORD your God will be with you wherever you go."*

Isaiah 41:13 (NIV) *For I am the LORD, your God, who takes hold of your right hand and says to you, "Do not fear; I will help you."*

REPENT	Jesus, I have allowed fear to mark my life and my relationship with you. I ask forgiveness for every way fear has affected my life, and the lives of those around me. I ask forgiveness for every way I have resisted you, denied your commands, and denied your character due to fear. (Specifically ask forgiveness for each box you checked, as well as any sins that come to mind associated with each category). I ask forgiveness for _____. I see it and call it sin. I now turn in repentance, committing myself to breaking the patterns of fear in my life.
RECEIVE	Jesus, I receive your forgiveness. I no longer fear that I am condemned by you, Jesus. I am washed by your blood, Jesus, and you loved me enough to sacrifice yourself for me.
REBUKE	In Jesus' name and authority, I rebuke every spirit of fear and command you to the feet of Jesus. In Jesus' name I rebuke every spirit that was given a foothold in my life due to fear. In the name of Jesus, every deceiving and lying spirit go to the feet of Jesus.
REPLACE	I replace the spirit of fear with the truth of who God is and who He created me to be.

APPLICATION:

Practice true repentance by confessing your fear openly. Fear will surely keep you from your destiny in Christ! Its job is to keep you frozen, and reliant on your own strength and abilities instead of living in faith. . .

(ENDNOTES) 1. "fear; decieve." *Merriam-Webster Online Dictionary.* 2007. http://www. merriam-webster.com (11 Jan. 2007)

PASSIVITY

Passivity can cause us to grow in our Christian life at a snail's pace. Not only will it hinder our growth, but it can literally cause us to move backward in our development. This is why our enemy wants passivity to remain hidden. We will have a powerful breakthrough in our life if we bring it out into the open! Passivity must be destroyed with force in the Christian life!

PASSIVITY: *It is the opposite of initiation. Passivity makes us move slowly and resists change and transformation. A good picture of passivity is the slowness of a turtle or sloth.*

RECOGNIZING PASSIVITY

James 4:17 (NIV) *Anyone, then, who knows the good he ought to do and doesn't do it, sins.*

Proverbs 20:4 (NIV) *A sluggard does not plow in season; so at harvest time he looks but finds nothing.*

Proverbs 10:4 (NIV) *Lazy hands make a man poor, but diligent hands bring wealth.*

Hebrews 6:11-12 (NIV) *We want each of you to show this same diligence to the very end, in order to make your hope sure. We do not want you to become lazy, but to imitate those who through faith and patience inherit what has been promised.*

Passivity is not from the Lord, and is a form of rebellion:

- It is the void left where action should be occurring.

- God calls us out of passivity. He calls us to be active in our faith, in building relationships, in service, and in every area of our lives.

Acts 20:34-35 (NLT) *You know that these hands of mine have worked to pay my own way, and I have even supplied the needs of those who were with me. And I have been a constant example of how you can help the poor by working hard. You should remember the words of the Lord Jesus: "It is more blessed to give than to receive."*

1 Corinthians 9:24-25 (NLT) *Remember that in a race everyone runs, but only one person gets the prize. You also must run in such a way that you will win. All athletes practice strict self-control. They do it to win a prize that will fade away, but we do it for an eternal prize.*

Colossians 3:23 (NLT) *Work hard and cheerfully at whatever you do, as though you were working for the Lord rather than for people.*

2 Timothy 2:6-7 (NLT) *Hardworking farmers are the first to enjoy the fruit of their labor. Think about what I am saying. The Lord will give you understanding in all these things.*

CHECK ALL THE BOXES THAT APPLY TO YOU:

1. Passivity is a lack of initiation.

- ❏ I walk in passivity when I fail to initiate conversations with others, always waiting for someone to come to me.
- ❏ I am passive in building relationships.
- ❏ I do not call others.
- ❏ I do not call people back when they call me (at least not right away).
- ❏ I do not initiate activities with others.
- ❏ At church or social gatherings, I tend to hang back until someone comes to talk to me.
- ❏ I do not affirm others; I withhold words of blessing.
- ❏ I do not protect others.
- ❏ I do not initiate growth in my relationship with the Lord.
- ❏ I cannot seem to motivate myself to read, pray, or worship.
- ❏ I feel no urgency or hunger in my relationship with God; I feel blocked (literally "locked down") when I consider spending time with Him.
- ❏ I feel content with where I am spiritually.
- ❏ I want to grow in the Lord, and I know what to do, but I do not do it.
- ❏ I know I need someone to pray with me for freedom in some areas, but I never get around to asking for help.
- ❏ Conversations with others about God do not push or motivate me.
- ❏ I do not initiate in serving others because I figure someone else will do it.
- ❏ I do not believe I can change the way I am.
- ❏ I often let others do what I could do myself.

2. Passivity is a form of independence and leads to isolation.

- ❏ I resist interdependence.
- ❏ I do not ask for help from the church body.
- ❏ I do not offer help/service to others in the church body.
- ❏ I see myself as more of a "private" Christian; I am reserved and keep to myself.
- ❏ I am critical of the way things are done in my church, and I have doubts about the leadership (I can see many flaws); it seems best for me to keep some distance and not get too involved.
- ❏ I tend to observe the activities of others (socially or in ministry); I rarely feel motivated or worthy to participate.
- ❏ I feel like I do not need anyone else.
- ❏ I feel unworthy to be in relationship with others.

3. Passivity is a form of resistance and rebellion.

- ❏ I resist God's forgiveness by not taking the authority Jesus has given me over my sin.
- ❏ I resist obedience to the Lord by allowing sin to remain in my life.
- ❏ I do not seek the place of repentance.
- ❏ I have become familiar with, and indifferent toward, sin in my life.
- ❏ I do not believe it would do any good to take authority over the enemy, so I rarely pray.
- ❏ I resist receiving the Lord's gifts.
- ❏ I do not believe that God will give me supernatural gifts and use them through me.
- ❏ I am not sure that spiritual gifts are authentic or for today; I want to keep a safe distance from them.
- ❏ I expect that others may receive spiritual gifts, but not me.
- ❏ I resist leadership positions, because I do not want that much responsibility or pressure.
- ❏ I do not like to do what everyone else does; I am my own person.
- ❏ It is not like me to get "more involved," and I do not want to be pressured to do so.
- ❏ It is not like me to be a leader or to be assertive.
- ❏ "If [that person] would just shut-up and let some others talk/lead/initiate once in a while, *then* maybe I would get involved (critical, judgmental spirit).

4. Passivity allows self-pity to remain.

- ❏ I am familiar with feelings like fear and rejection, so I tend to believe that I will always struggle in these areas.
- ❏ I am comfortable with the way I am.
- ❏ I am a victim; I do not know how *not* to be a victim.
- ❏ Others are wrong to push me to become someone I am not.
- ❏ I blame others for the way that I am.

5. Passivity is about being too comfortable.

- ❏ I allow myself to be comfortable with where I am spiritually. I am alright with my walk with God right now.
- ❏ I allow myself to be comfortable with where I am emotionally. I have *always* struggled with depression, insecurity, shyness, fear, loneliness, etc. This is the way things are, so why should I worry about it and try to find a "cure?"
- ❏ I allow myself to be comfortable with where I am physically. I do not care what others think of my appearance. It is too bad if they do not like what they see; I do not need them anyway.

6. Passivity perpetuates lies and deceptions.

- ❑ This is part of my personality.
- ❑ I am not meant to step out and initiate or I would really feel like it.
- ❑ I will be a failure if I try to initiate.
- ❑ It is just not me!
- ❑ There is nothing wrong with me, so I do not need to seek change or freedom.
- ❑ At least there is *some* comfort in self-pity and being a victim.
- ❑ I do not need anyone to tell me how to act!

READ THIS BEFORE YOU PRAY

It is important to realize that we are praying spiritual warfare prayers! A spiritual warfare prayer can often be loud and forceful; wars are not fought in silence. Is there such a thing as a silent battleship? Do you know of a tank that fires its weapons in silence? Can a bomb be detonated without an explosion? This is why part of the "basic training" of this class is learning to pray spiritual warfare prayers.

Remember, your greatest weapon in this battle is repentance; the deeper the repentance, the greater the advancement. Shouting or jumping will never destroy a stronghold. However, true repentance combined with using your authority in Jesus Christ will *always* overcome a stronghold. Strongholds are not built overnight, and this is why we need to learn how to *pray and obey!* You probably checked a few boxes on the worksheet, and now we are going to practice praying authoritative prayers.

Passivity is a spirit that wants to keep your mouth shut and your influence held captive. It does not want you to rise up! It does not want you to pray and discover the authority that Jesus has given you! It does not want you to radically bless those around you!

Jesus wants you to discover the wonderful gift of repentance as it is described in Scripture. We are surely remorseful for our sin, but the Lord has won the battle and paid the price. Jesus wants you to discover that repentance can be a joy!

After you are done repenting, rebuke the enemy and pray the following Scriptures out loud. We are declaring from deep within us the opposite of passivity.

WALKING IN THE OPPOSITE SPIRIT

- ☑ Initiate conversations, activities, etc. with others. Go to them—do not wait for them to come to you.
- ☑ Even when you do not "feel like it," take authority over sin patterns such as self-pity and victimization. Do not allow sin to remain. You have authority—use it!
- ☑ Doing things when you really do not feel like it is the whole point of walking in the opposite spirit. Here is the lie: If you do not feel like it, you do not have to do anything. <u>Do</u> what you <u>know</u> to do—whether you feel like it or not!
- ☑ Go out of your way to bless people.
- ☑ Begin to cry out to God for a greater hunger to grow spiritually.

REPENT	Lord Jesus, I ask forgiveness for patterns of <u>passivity</u> in my life. I see how it has affected me and those around me. I call it sin. Passivity is not from you! (Go back and confess each specific box you checked). I repent of every way that passivity has been in my life, and I commit to breaking the patterns of passivity in my life, right now!
RECEIVE	Lord Jesus, I now receive your forgiveness for walking in passivity. I accept your offering of cleansing from this sin and I believe that I am forgiven! I no longer resist your healing, but I freely accept it.
REBUKE	I rebuke you, passivity, for attacking me with lies about my true nature and calling, causing me to be passive in many areas of my life! I come against you by the authority of Jesus Christ within me, and I command you to flee <u>right now</u>! You are a liar and I will no longer listen to you and your deceptions about me! I put you under my feet, according to the Word of God, and I crush you and the influence you have had in my life.
REPLACE	I replace the spirit of passivity with the truth of who God is and who He created me to be.

THEMES OF SCRIPTURE TO DECLARE

"I will walk after the Lord my God and fear Him, and keep His commandments and obey His voice; I shall serve Him and hold fast to Him."
from Deuteronomy 13:4

"I am the salt and light of the earth!"
from Matthew 5:13-14

"I have been chosen and appointed to bear fruit!"
from John 15:16

"I am God's co-worker!"
from 2 Corinthians 6:1

"I can do all things through Christ who strengthens me!"
from Philippians 4:13

"I am established, anointed and sealed by God!"
from 2 Corinthians 1:21-22

"I have not been given a spirit of timidity, but of power, love and self-discipline."
from 2 Timothy 1:7

"I am not lazy, but I imitate those who through faith and patience inherit what has been promised!"
from Hebrews 6:11-12

APPLICATION:

Pray against passivity now! Passivity has come to steal the joy of living a fruitful Christian life. Rise up and confess this sin and drive it out of your life.

Take time this week to walk in the opposite direction. In whatever area you have been most passive—do the exact opposite. It is so fun and exciting to agree with God about who you are! You are a leader! You are bold in Christ! You are the light of the world!

NOTES:

REJECTION

DIRECTIONS FOR HOW TO USE THIS MATERIAL

The Rejection, Unforgiveness, and Anger worksheets are to be used together in the following ways:

1. Read and study the material on the stronghold of rejection.

2. Then read and study the material on the stronghold of unforgiveness.

3. Once both of these studies are complete, use the Anger Worksheet to actually walk through the process of granting and receiving forgiveness. The Anger Worksheet is designed to walk through the practical steps of addressing those issues uncovered by reading and studying the material on rejection and unforgiveness.

INTRODUCTION

Romans 5:4b-5 (NLT) *Our confident expectation of salvation will not disappoint us. For we know how dearly God loves us, because He has given us the Holy Spirit to fill our hearts with His love.*

We belong to a society that values winning and worships winners. We live in a world system that chooses favorites and rejects seconds. We learn, nearly from birth, that the most popular, the most attractive, and the most talented are "in." Those who do not fit that description (most of us) are "out." And so, even before a specific action or attitude presents itself, the stage has been set for each of us to live life battling rejection.

Rejection is foundational to many strongholds, sins, and dysfunctions. *This is because rejection affects our entire personality.* It not only tears down an individual, but it infiltrates all relationships: marriage, family, ministry, work, and friends. The stage for rejection has already been set by the world system, which we know to be under the direction of Satan himself, the "accuser of the brethren" (Revelation 12:10). We yearn for love and acceptance, but instead receive rejection. We learn to believe the lies forced on us about our own value, our own significance, and the love of God, who is our Heavenly Father.

However, if we are in Christ, we do not need to be held captive to the way the world thinks. We are not of this world (Ephesians 2:12-13; Philippians 3:20; Hebrews 11:13-16; 1 Peter 2:11). **We have not been rejected; we have been ACCEPTED** (Romans 15:7). There is *NOTHING* that can separate us from the love of our Father (Romans 8:38-39). *We must not agree with the lies of the world any longer!* Instead, we must face those lies squarely, identify what they are and where they come from, and utterly destroy them with the sword of the Spirit—the Word of God.

ROOTS OF REJECTION

- Absentee fathers or mothers.
- Lack of bonding with parents.
- Parents' divorce.
- Not being wanted as a child; "wrong" gender; blamed for your parent's problems.
- Adoption.
- Competition with brothers and sisters.
- Various forms of abuse (physical, emotional, sexual).
- Parents' addictions.
- Shame of a family member; because someone in your family did something it brought rejection from others. An alcoholic parent could be an example.
- Constant fighting or strife.
- Unjust discipline.
- Parents' disinterest in a child's activities.
- Various means and degrees of neglect/abandonment.
- Having or contributing toward an abortion.
- Mistreating another person.
- Addictions.
- Living with a physical defect or handicap.
- Discontent with one's appearance.
- Sense of failure or inadequacy; lack of confidence in abilities.
- Infidelity of a spouse.
- Divorce.
- Breaking off of an engagement or other significant relationship.
- Loss of valued employment.
- Betrayal by a close friend.
- Unexpected, premature death of a loved one.
- Spiritual abuse, hurt, or betrayal in a church.

FRUITS OF REJECTION (emotional responses)

Check all the boxes that apply to you:

1. **Nervousness.**
    - ❑ I talk over others; interrupting. I fear not being heard or understood.
    - ❑ I experience nervous physical activity, including inability to rest without activity.
    - ❑ I am impatient with my personal growth and the growth of others.

2. **Pursuing Comfort.**
    - ❑ Lust.
    - ❑ Procrastination.

- ❑ I delay taking responsibility. I delay discipline.
- ❑ I live for "the weekend" or for sport.

3. **Social Awkwardness**
    - ❑ I am fearful and nervous in social situations.
    - ❑ I gravitate toward those who are shy or inadequate.
    - ❑ I communicate with others in guarded and general terms.
    - ❑ I leave times with others wishing I had spoken or behaved differently.

4. **Inability to accept self.**
    - ❑ I am constantly preoccupied and discouraged over my appearance.
    - ❑ I am discouraged over my personal weaknesses.
    - ❑ I am unable to fully appreciate what God has created me to be and do.
    - ❑ I either downplay or boast in my abilities.
    - ❑ I am unable to truly acknowledge or celebrate others' victories.
    - ❑ I am jealous, and I envy the desirable qualities of others.
    - ❑ I am extremely hard on myself.
    - ❑ I become angry at the thought of past rejection, then blame myself.

5. **Critical attitude toward others.**
    - ❑ I do not fully trust others.
    - ❑ I hold others and their motivation suspect.
    - ❑ I am immediately skeptical of new people; they must prove themselves.
    - ❑ I focus on others' weaknesses.
    - ❑ I have a "wait and see" attitude about others' ability to change.

6. **What is wrong with me?**
    - ❑ I feel that there is something innately wrong with me.
    - ❑ I hate myself because of past rejection.
    - ❑ I must be what people say because I keep getting rejected.

7. **Isolation.**
    - ❑ I am not a "people person."
    - ❑ I feel like I would be better off alone.
    - ❑ I have a strong desire to get time alone.
    - ❑ Interaction with others is stressful for me.

8. Loneliness.

- ❑ I experience sorrow and depression over being alone.
- ❑ I believe that no one will ever accept me for who I am.
- ❑ I fear that I will never have meaningful long-term relationships.

9. Temporal Values.

- ❑ I often say, "If I only had _____ then I would be _____."
- ❑ I focus on material possessions for satisfaction.
- ❑ I search for satisfaction through others' approval.
- ❑ I am concerned with position, or place in life.
- ❑ I feel if I tried harder, then people would accept me.
- ❑ I believe that if life was "perfect" then the sting of rejection would leave.

10. Self-Pity.

- ❑ I believe that I am not loved by anyone, even God.
- ❑ Everyone is disappointed with me, even God.
- ❑ I feel that I just can't get it together.

11. Defensiveness.

- ❑ If others don't like me that's their problem.
- ❑ I blame others for my state of mind.
- ❑ I see correction as an attack, and react harshly.

12. Numbness and Resignation.

- ❑ I react with apathy toward physical or verbal abuse.
- ❑ I feel like I can never do anything right, so why try?
- ❑ I feel like I have crossed the line; so what does it matter anymore?
- ❑ I am unable or refuse to have emotion.
- ❑ I give up on areas of personal holiness (drugs, drinking, sexual relationships).

RECOGNIZING REJECTION

- ❑ I usually interpret things that could be either positive or negative as negative.
- ❑ I receive what others say to me through a lens of rejection.
- ❑ I am assaulted with paralyzing thoughts such as, "I can't do that!" "How would that appear to _____?" "What would _____ think?"
- ❑ I second-guess what I have said or done and I have negative thoughts about what others must think about me as a result.

- ❑ I find it difficult to freely reach out and exercise my spiritual gifts.
- ❑ I often try to do too much or go from activity to activity, job to job, or ministry to ministry, striving to earn favor and acceptance from God and/or others.
- ❑ I find it difficult to accept praise and encouragement freely from others or to demonstrate love and affection.
- ❑ I do not believe people when they pay me a compliment.
- ❑ I have a tendency to doubt, to question, or to mistrust authority.
- ❑ I tend to be skeptical and unbelieving.
- ❑ People could describe me as harsh.
- ❑ I struggle to control foul language and abusive speech, especially when I am angry.
- ❑ When confronted about something, my immediate reaction is defensive or even defiant.
- ❑ I do not share my testimony or the Gospel, with the unsaved.
- ❑ I am afraid that I, or my loved ones, have not been chosen by God for salvation.
- ❑ I need to control my family in order for them to be safe, to succeed, and so they will love and appreciate me.
- ❑ I am possessive in relationships.
- ❑ I have a low estimation of my own appearance, my abilities, and my adequacy to succeed in life and ministry.
- ❑ I am prone to depression.
- ❑ I am often fearful and anxious about things, such as how people regard me or my children, how my efforts (or another's) will turn out, and how I will be provided for and protected, etc.
- ❑ I need to be needed, so I continually place myself in situations where I feel others cannot get along without my help, my presence, my abilities, my ministry, etc.
- ❑ I am inhibited in honestly sharing my deepest feelings with others, even with those who are close to me.
- ❑ I am afraid that if I am vulnerable with my wife, I will appear weak and lose my place of authority and respect in her eyes.
- ❑ I am afraid that if I am vulnerable with my husband, he will take advantage of me and exploit my weaknesses.
- ❑ I am both critical and envious at the same time toward others who are more confident, who are able to express themselves freely, or who have more friendships and opportunities than *I think* I do.
- ❑ I am competitive and ambitious. I think that if people will not love me at least they will admire me.
- ❑ I find comfort in isolation; others might consider me a "loner."

FALSE REJECTION

The rejection issues noted prior have their roots in reality; the offenses that created the sense of rejection really did happen. Two forms of rejection that are *not* based in reality are *perceived* rejection and *feared* rejection. These are pure demonic lies that convince a person that rejection is present, or pending, when it is not. This can paralyze us in life, strip us of joy, and compel us to always be on guard against what others may be thinking.

GOD'S "COPING MECHANISM"

When we are faced with the fear of rejection, the temptation is to fall back on *coping mechanisms* we may have employed for most—if not all—of our lives. These can include anything we have learned to use or to do to comfort ourselves in the face of rejection or other hurts. We should recognize our coping mechanisms as false comforts. Like a placebo, they trick us into thinking we have dealt with the symptoms of our pain, when in truth, they do nothing to solve the problem.

Steps to take:

1. **Grant forgiveness and extend blessings to people who have hurt or rejected you (real or perceived).** Do the same toward situations and environments from which hurt and rejection continue to flow. Remember that Satan wants to stimulate bitterness, resentment, and anger in you. Our refusal to forgive becomes a cancer that defiles not only us, but also many around us. This is why the Scriptures repeatedly address the issue of granting forgiveness.

   Matthew 6:12, 14-15 (NIV) *Forgive us our debts, as we also have forgiven our debtors. For if you forgive men when they sin against you, your heavenly Father will also forgive you. But if you do not forgive men their sins, your Father will not forgive your sins.*

Romans 12:20-21 (NIV) *On the contrary: "If your enemy is hungry, feed him; if he is thirsty, give him something to drink. In doing this, you will heap burning coals on his head." Do not be overcome by evil, but overcome evil with good.*

Ephesians 3:31-32; 5:1 (NIV) *Get rid of all bitterness, rage and anger, brawling and slander, along with every form of malice. Be kind and compassionate to one another, forgiving each other, just as in Christ God forgave you. Be imitators of God, therefore, as dearly loved children and live a life of love, just as Christ loved us and gave himself up for us as a fragrant offering and sacrifice to God.*

2. **Be confident of God's great, unconditional and infinite love for you.** God did not make a mistake when He made you! His great love is demonstrated through Jesus' death on the cross and through His continual faithfulness and devotion to you. As you reject and demolish any strongholds and demonic lies of rejection, replace them with the truth of God's great love for you.

   1 John 3:1 (NIV) *How great is the love the Father has lavished on us, that we should be called children of God! And that is what we are!*

3. **Live in these truths.** This means acting on faith, not feelings! It means behaving lovingly and confidently even when we fear people will reject us: parents, friends, children, co-workers, neighbors, and church family. It means forgiving and moving forward, even if people do reject us.

   1 John 4:15-18 (NIV) *If anyone acknowledges that Jesus is the Son of God, God lives in him and he in God. And so we know and rely on the love God has for us. God is love. Whoever lives in love lives in God, and God in him. In this way, love is made complete among us so that we will have confidence on the day of judgment, because in this world we are like him. There is no fear in love. But perfect love drives out fear, because fear has to do with punishment. The one who fears is not made perfect in love.*

WALKING IN THE TRUTH

To walk out of rejection you must immerse yourself in the truth of God's word about who you really are. You need to think about how much He loves you, accepts you, and demonstrates His faithfulness to you. Do not accept the lies of the enemy, perhaps planted into your mind and reinforced since childhood, that you are unloved, unaccepted, unworthy, and rejected.

Speak these truths out loud from your heart:

❑ I will treat other people according to the truth of God's word, not on the basis of my own fears, hurts, and insecurities: I will forgive, I will extend blessing, and I will freely love and accept others.

❑ I will offer encouragement, blessing, and affection to others.

❑ I will express my thoughts and feelings to others honestly, without fear of rejection.

❑ I will no longer resort to rebellion to express my anger over feeling rejected.

❑ I will no longer try to "do" for others so they will love and accept me. I will minister with my spiritual gifts according to the direction and power of the Holy Spirit.

❑ I will not fear weakness and vulnerability with my spouse. I will trust God to support me.

❑ I will not be critical of those who I feel have rejected me, or those who I regard as walking in greater freedom, acceptance, or confidence than me.

❑ I will form attitudes, initiate actions, and speak words that will comfort and encourage others.

❑ I will not seek comfort in self-pity or isolation.

❑ I will be myself, enjoying and becoming more comfortable with how God made me.

❑ I will share my faith in Jesus Christ whenever and with whomever, the Holy Spirit gives opportunity.

SCRIPTURE TO REFLECT UPON

Psalm 13:1, 5-6 (NIV) *How long, O Lord? Will you forget me forever? How long will you hide your face from me? But I trust in your unfailing love; my heart rejoices in your salvation. I will sing to the Lord because he has been so good to me.*

Psalm 27:1, 10 (NIV) *The Lord is my light and my salvation —whom shall I fear? The Lord is the stronghold of my life —of whom shall I be afraid? Though my father and mother forsake me, the Lord will receive me.*

Psalm 48:9 (NIV) *Within your temple, O God, we meditate on your unfailing love.*

Psalm 66:20 (NIV) *Praise be to God, who has not rejected my prayer or withheld his love from me!*

Psalm 147:3 (NIV) *He heals the brokenhearted and binds up their wounds.*

Isaiah 41:9-10 (NIV) *I took you from the ends of the earth, from its farthest corners I called you. I said, "You are my servant;" I have chosen you and have not rejected you. So do not fear, for I am with you; do not be dismayed, for I am your God. I will strengthen you and help you; I will uphold you with my righteous right hand.*

Isaiah 53:3-5 (NIV) *He was despised and rejected by men, a man of sorrows, and familiar with suffering. Like one from whom men hide their faces he was despised, and we esteemed him not. Surely he took up our infirmities and carried our sorrows, yet we considered him stricken by God, smitten by him, and afflicted. But he was pierced for our transgressions, he was crushed for our iniquities; the punishment that brought us peace was upon him, and by his wounds we are healed.*

Isaiah 54:10 (NIV) *"Though the mountains be shaken and the hills be removed, yet my unfailing love for you will not be shaken nor my covenant of peace be removed," says the Lord, who has compassion on you.*

Lamentations 3:22 (NIV) *Because of the Lord's great love we are not consumed, for his compassions never fail. They are new every morning; great is your faithfulness.*

Romans 5:8 (NIV) *But God demonstrated his own love for us in this: While we were still sinners, Christ died for us.*

Zephaniah 3:17 (NIV) *The LORD your God is with you, he is mighty to save. He will take great delight in you, he will quiet you with his love, he will rejoice over you with singing.*

Romans 8:38-39 (NIV) *For I am convinced that neither death nor life, neither angels nor demons, neither the present nor the future, nor any powers, neither height nor depth, nor anything else in all creation, will be able to separate us from the love of God that is in Christ Jesus our Lord.*

Ephesians 1:4-6 (NIV) *For he chose us in him before the creation of the world to be holy and blameless in his sight. In love he predestined us to be adopted as his sons through Jesus Christ, in accordance with his pleasure and will—to the praise of his glorious grace, which he has freely given us in the One he loves.*

Ephesians 2:4-7 (NIV) *But because of his great love for us, God, who is rich in mercy, made us alive with Christ even when we were dead in transgressions—it is by grace you have been saved. And God raised us up with Christ and seated us with him in the heavenly realms in Christ Jesus, in order that in the coming ages he might show the incomparable riches of his grace, expressed in his kindness to us in Christ Jesus.*

Ephesians 3:17b-19 (NIV) *And I pray that you, being rooted and established in love, may have power, together with all the saints, to grasp how wide and long and high and deep is the love of Christ, and to know this love that surpasses knowledge—that you may be filled to the measure of all the fullness of God.*

1 Peter 2:4-7 (NIV) *As you come to him, the living Stone —rejected by men but chosen by God and precious to him —you also, like living stones, are being built into a spiritual house to be a holy priesthood, offering spiritual sacrifices acceptable to God through Jesus Christ. For in Scripture it says: "See, I lay a stone in Zion, a chosen and precious cornerstone, and the one who trusts in him will never be put to shame." Now to you who believe, this stone is precious. But to those who do not believe, "The stone the builders rejected has become the capstone …"*

1 John 3:1 (NIV) *How great is the love the Father has lavished on us, that we should be called children of God! And that is what we are!*

1 John 4:9-10 (NIV) *This is how God showed his love among us: He sent his one and only Son into the world that we might live through him. This is love: not that we loved God, but that he loved us and sent his Son as an atoning sacrifice for our sins.*

BREAKING INTO FREEDOM FROM REJECTION

In the past, when you were hurt or fearful, you gave in to your natural, self-defensive coping mechanisms instead of turning to the Lord to comfort and defend you. This was sin—and an open invitation to the enemy of our souls. The apostle Paul wrote that he had learned to *"put no confidence in the flesh"* (Philippians 3:3). Can you say the same? That is walking in freedom!

The *opposite* of depending on our own coping mechanisms (false comforts) is *faith*. Faith is believing God—that He is who He says He is, that He will do what He says He will do, and that you are who He says you are.

- He is sovereign.
- He is love.
- He is just.
- He is wise.
- He will comfort.
- He will defend.
- He will protect.
- He will provide.
- You are His much-loved child.
- You are filled with the Holy Spirit.
- You have the authority of Jesus Christ.
- You have nothing to fear.

DESTROYING FALSE COMFORT

When new (or old) hurts, insecurities, fears, and difficulties arise, do not succumb to an automatic reaction to turn back to old false comforts. Look at the attack through *spiritual* eyes, and see it for what it is. What is the enemy's scheme? What false comfort am I tempted to seek? Do not forget:

- False comforts are thoughts, attitudes, and behaviors that help us cope with emotional pain. They are not based on truth, and are not of God's Holy Spirit.
- False comforts can be material, emotional, physical, or spiritual.
- False comforts are really a form of idolatry (Isaiah 30:1-13; 31:1-9; 1 Corinthians 10:1-14; 1 John 5:18-21).
- When faced with temptation (such as fear of rejection), you will be presented with two options: 1. God's comfort (requires faith, obedience, courage, and truth) or 2. false comfort (which is the most natural reaction).
- When you choose God's comfort (i.e., forgiving and blessing), you operate with increased levels of faith, authority, and the power of the Holy Spirit.
- Identify and grant forgiveness and blessing to *any* offender(s), real or perceived. This may take you all the way back to your childhood! The Holy Spirit will not overwhelm you; He will bring to mind only what you need for the moment.

DO NOT FORGET THESE:

- ☑ **REPENT** and ask forgiveness of any and all attitudes and actions associated with *rejection*.

- ☑ **RECEIVE** forgiveness from the Lord. Receive the infilling and empowering work of the Holy Spirit. Seek it and depend on it at all times; determine not to settle for false comforts! Receive the work that God has done and is doing in you (and live in it) in faith!

- ☑ **REBUKE** and renounce the lies and influences related to *rejection*.

- ☑ **REPLACE** lies with truth, confidence, and **security in God's love for you**, continually renewing your mind with His word and in His spirit.

NOTES:

+definition+

SHAME:
[noun] **1a:** a painful emotion caused by consciousness of guilt, shortcoming, or impropriety. **1b:** the susceptibility to such emotion. **2:** a condition of humiliating disgrace or disrepute. [1]

RECOGNIZING SHAME

1. <u>Shame is not from God.</u>
   Psalm 25:3 (NIV) *No one whose hope is in you will ever be put to shame . . .*

2. <u>Shame is a result of sin.</u>
   Proverbs 13:18 (NIV) *He who ignores discipline comes to poverty and shame.*

   Jeremiah 8:9 (NIV) *The wise will be put to shame . . . since they have rejected the word of the Lord.*

   Genesis 3:6-7 (NLT) *The woman was convinced. The fruit looked so fresh and delicious, and it would make her so wise! So she ate some of the fruit. She also gave*

some to her husband, who was with her. Then he ate it, too. At that moment, their eyes were opened, and they suddenly felt shame at their nakedness. So they strung fig leaves together around their hips to cover themselves.

Check all the boxes that apply to you:

1. **Shame causes us to develop shallow and guarded relationships.**

   ❑ I am afraid others might find out about this sin.

   ❑ I have trouble forming trusting relationships because I guard against getting "too personal" with others.

   ❑ I am very fearful that others can see my ugly sin; this causes me to fear getting close to anyone, including God.

   ❑ I live in constant fear that others will reject me if this sin is discovered.

2. **Shame results in a continuous battle with self-condemnation.**

   ❑ I struggle with inferiority.

   ❑ I tend to think negatively about myself, and I battle negative thoughts about myself continuously.

   ❑ When I compare myself to others, I almost always "lose" in the comparison.

   ❑ I beat myself up continually because of my past.

3. **Shame brings deep feelings of guilt and unworthiness; this, in turn, leads to self-hatred.**
   - ❑ I feel dirty, ruined; like damaged goods.
   - ❑ I have trouble finding intimacy with God because I feel so far from Him.
   - ❑ I seem unable to forgive myself.
   - ❑ I feel that I could never marry a godly man/woman because he/she might find out about this sin and reject me.
   - ❑ I do not believe I can lead others because this sin has made me unworthy.
   - ❑ I hate myself. I do not blame others for not wanting to be friends with me; I do not deserve their friendship anyway.

4. **Shame brings constant reminders of this sin.**
   - ❑ I cannot stop thinking about this!
   - ❑ I constantly fight off disturbing memories of my shameful experience(s).
   - ❑ I have disturbing dreams and visions about this sin.

5. **Shame robs us of the joy of forgiveness and blocks the Lord's healing.**
   - ❑ I do not feel I can be forgiven for this sin.
   - ❑ It is hard for me to believe that God can forgive even *this*.
   - ❑ I cannot tell anyone about this, including God, because it is so shameful.

6. **Deceptions and lies.**
   - ❑ No one else has ever committed a sin as bad as this one.
   - ❑ I cannot tell *anyone* about this sin because they will reject me.
   - ❑ I will never be clean.
   - ❑ I will never be able to have deep relationships with others because I must make sure they never learn the truth about this sin.
   - ❑ This pattern of shame will always be a part of my life. There will never be lasting victory. I will fall right back into this pattern.

AREAS OF SHAME
(Some areas where shame can be hidden.)

1. **Regret.**
   - ❑ "I can't believe I did that."

   - ❑ My mind is consumed with a specific event.
   - ❑ I cringe at the thought of a specific act.

2. **Failure.**
   - ❑ Failed jobs.
   - ❑ Failed marriage(s).
   - ❑ Failed entrepreneurial work.
   - ❑ Failed education.
   - ❑ Failed relationship with children.
   - ❑ Failed relationship with parents.

3. **Personal embarrassment over:**
   - ❑ Social standing.
   - ❑ Personal state of my children.
   - ❑ What I have achieved in life.
   - ❑ The behavior of my spouse.
   - ❑ Watching alcoholic or drug addicted parents embarrass themselves.
   - ❑ Where I have come from; my background.

4. **Defeat over:**
   - ❑ Hidden addiction(s).
   - ❑ Unconfessed sin(s).
   - ❑ A stronghold I do not have victory over.
   - ❑ Unconfessed affair(s).
   - ❑ Unconfessed abortion(s).
   - ❑ Unconfessed abuse(s) of which you were either a perpetrator or a victim.

SIDEBAR

GODLY SORROW VS. REGRET

2 Corinthians 7:10 (NIV) *Godly sorrow brings repentance that leads to salvation and leaves no regret, but worldly sorrow brings death.*

REMEMBER:

Condemnation is not of God. It is a tool of the enemy. It says, "There is no light at the end of the tunnel." Condemnation, or "worldly sorrow," leads to regret and death.

Godly sorrow or remorse, leads to repentance and life. It is the instruction and correction of a loving father who knows what is best for you.

SHAME RELATED TO SINFUL CHOICES

1. Drug use.

The Greek word **pharmakeia** {/far·mak·i·ah/} has three biblical occurrences. The King James Version translates it as "sorcery" twice, and "witchcraft" once: 1. The use or the administering of drugs. 2. Poisoning. 3. Sorcery, magical arts; often found in connection with idolatry and fostered by it. [2]

Steps to take:

1. Ask the Lord to forgive you for each type of drug you have used. It is important to speak the name of the drug out loud so that all the hidden shame can be eradicated.
2. Ask the Lord to forgive the activities that you participated in while you were on each drug.
3. If you sold drugs, ask the Lord to forgive you.
4. Ask the Lord to forgive you for participating in witchcraft by taking drugs.
5. Receive His forgiveness.

2. Rebellion.

The Scriptures reveal that there is a close association between rebellion and witchcraft. The following verse demonstrates this for us:

1 Samuel 15:23 (NKJV) *For rebellion is as the sin of witchcraft, And stubbornness is as iniquity and idolatry*

Rebellion is defined as, "opposition to one in authority or dominance."[3] Rebellion can exist in attitudes, words, and actions and can manifest in diverse forms. It can be aggressive or passive; it is expressed through defiance and/or disobedience; it is demonstrated through insubordination or insurrection.

God says that it is as witchcraft because Satan's kingdom is built on rebellion. He led an insurrection against God and His authority, but it was a colossal failure. Satan and the angels who followed him were overcome and sentenced to intense eternal judgment.

Sometimes extremely shameful activity comes out of the sin of rebellion. Lives are filled with regret, guilt, self-hatred, sorrow, and shame as a result of rebellious choices (the Freedom 2 book gives a more extensive teaching on rebellion for further study).

3. Formal Witchcraft.

Formal witchcraft is an increasing part of the culture in Western Civilization. There is a growing interest in witchcraft related books, movies, and games. But even beyond these forms of "entertainment" there is a larger population participating in more sophisticated activities such as Wicca, or even the deep witchcraft activities of rituals, incantations, hexes, etc. Witchcraft has long been practiced openly in the African, Asian, and Latin American cultures.

Many lives are destroyed and, as a result, many individuals will war with shame from involvement in formal witchcraft.

Witchcraft includes direct experimentation and involvement in the occult, including participation in false religions, demonic forms of entertainment including horror movies, demonic games (and the rituals associated with them), and demonic video/computer games.

Deuteronomy 18:9-14 (NIV) *When you enter the land which the LORD your God gives you, you shall not learn to imitate the detestable things of those nations. There shall not be found among you anyone who makes his son or his daughter pass through the fire, one who uses divination, one who practices witchcraft, or one who interprets omens, or a sorcerer, or one who casts a spell, or a medium, or a spiritist, or one who calls up the dead. For whoever does these things is detestable to the LORD; and because of these detestable things the LORD your God will drive them out before you. You shall be blameless before the LORD your God. For those nations, which you shall dispossess, listen to those who practice witchcraft and to diviners, but as for you, the LORD your God has not allowed you to do so.*

Romans 16:19 (NLT) *But everyone knows that you are obedient to the Lord. This makes me very happy. I want you to see clearly what is right and to stay innocent of any wrong.*

Steps to take:

1. Ask the Lord to forgive you for the sin of rebellion and witchcraft.
2. Ask the Lord to forgive you for each specific activity in which you participated.
3. Renounce all curses/words that agreed with Satan's kingdom.
4. Remove accursed objects you have been associated with:

> **2 Corinthians 6:17 (NIV)** *"Therefore come out from them and be separate," says the Lord. "Touch no unclean thing, and I will receive you."*

> **Deuteronomy 7:25-26 (NASB)** *The graven images of their gods you are to burn with fire; you shall not covet the silver or the gold that is on them, nor take it for yourselves, or you will be snared by it, for it is an abomination to the Lord your God. You shall not bring an abomination into your house, and like it come under the ban; you shall utterly detest it and you shall utterly abhor it, for it is something banned.*

Steps to take with accursed objects:

a. Throw away or destroy the objects: games, music, articles, books, movies, etc., that are in agreement with Satan's kingdom.
b. Ask the Lord to forgive all idolatry and sever all curses associated with the item. Sever all words that you may have sung to music that was in agreement with Satan's kingdom (2 Corinthians 6:14-18).

4. **Sexual Sin**
Because sexual sin affects our own body, you open yourself up to shame and self condemnation. It is common to have a difficult time forgiving yourself for sexual sin. Secret habits and or addictions are just that—secret. These forms are designed by the enemy to not only satisfy lusts, but to create shameful isolation.

> **James 5:16 (NIV)** *Therefore confess your sins to each other and pray for each other so that you may be healed.*

> **1 Corinthians 6:14-20 (NIV)** *The body is not meant for sexual immorality, but for the Lord, and the Lord for the body. By his power God raised the Lord from the dead, and he will raise us also. Do you not know that your bodies are members of Christ himself? Shall I then take the members of Christ and unite them with a prostitute? Never! Do you not know that he who unites himself with a prostitute is one with her in body? For it is said, "The two will become one flesh." But he who unites himself*

with the Lord is one with him in spirit. Flee from sexual immorality. All other sins a man commits are outside his body, but he who sins sexually sins against his own body. Do you not know that your body is a temple of the Holy Spirit, who is in you, whom you have received from God? You are not your own; you were bought at a price. Therefore honor God with your body.

Areas of sexual sin to ask forgiveness for:

1. Fornication (sex prior to marriage).
2. Pornography.
3. Childhood experimentation (acts that were done while growing up).
4. Fantasy.
5. Any other acts of sexual sin.
6. Sever all soul ties with any person that you had sex with prior to marriage. (Soul ties are referenced in the Anger worksheet in the homework section.)

Note: Shame will keep its hold on us as long as we are afraid to specifically name the sins that brought shame. Before proceeding through the 4 R's, confess each area to one person. Do not hold anything back. Make sure men confess to men and women confess to women. Because self-hatred is often a part of shame, ask God's forgiveness for self-hatred. When you have taken these steps, move on to the 4-R's. (Remember, the deeper the repentance, the greater the freedom!)

WALKING IN THE OPPOSITE SPIRIT

☑ Meditate on the promises of God about perfect forgiveness. This will weaken the lies that accuse you of being "unclean." They will be a source of comfort, as well as a reminder of your true standing before the Lord.

☑ Set your sights high: You are worthy of deep and lasting relationships, including a healthy marriage to a wonderful man/woman of God!

REPENT	Lord Jesus, I ask for your forgiveness for shame. I repent of all the ways I have allowed shame to be a part of my life. I see how it has affected me and others around me. I name it as sin. Shame is not from you! (Go back through the boxes you checked and ask God to forgive you in each area.)
RECEIVE	Lord Jesus, I now receive your forgiveness for carrying shame. I accept your offering of cleansing from this sin and I say that I am forgiven! I no longer resist your healing; instead, I choose to accept it freely.
REBUKE	I rebuke you, Satan, for attacking me with thoughts of shame, disgrace, and unworthiness! I come against you by the authority of Jesus Christ, and I command you to flee right now! You are a liar, and I will no longer listen to you and your deceptions about me! According to the Word of God, I put you under my feet right now and I crush you and the influence you have had in my life.
REPLACE	I replace the deception of the enemy with the truth of Scripture. I make these declarations based on the Word of God with zeal! "I, who trust in Him, will never be put to shame" (Romans 9:33). "My hope is in You so I will never be put to shame" (Psalm 25:3). "If I humble myself and pray and seek Your face and turn from my wicked ways, then You will hear from heaven and will forgive my sin and will heal me" (2 Chronicles 7:14). "I look to You and I am radiant; my face is never covered with shame" (Psalm 34:5). "You will give me a new heart and put a new spirit in me; You will remove my heart of stone and give me a heart of flesh" (Ezekiel 36:26). "Therefore there is now no condemnation for me, for I am in Christ Jesus" (Romans 8:1). "I will praise the name of the Lord my God, who has worked wonders for me; never again will I be ashamed" (Joel 2:26). "I am God's workmanship, created in Christ Jesus to do good works, which God has prepared in advance for me to do" (Ephesians 2:10). "I have been redeemed and forgiven of all my sins" (Colossians 1:14).

APPLICATION:

Immediate prayer time: *It is time to live a life without the weight of shame and constant guilt.* The sorrow of your past can weigh you down so that you cannot enjoy your future. The devil will accuse you until you can honestly say, "I have dealt with all of that at the cross and shame and regret has no place in my life!"

Break down into small groups with a leader and walk through asking forgiveness for all unconfessed sins that cause you to live in shame.

(ENDNOTES)

1. "shame." *Merriam-Webster Online Dictionary.* 2007. http://www.merriam-webster. com (11 Jan. 2007).

2. James Strong. *The Exhaustive Concordance of the Bible:* (electronic ed.) (Woodside Bible Fellowship.: Ontario, 1996)

3. "rebellion." *Merriam-Webster Online Dictionary.* 2007. http://www.merriam-webster.com (11 Jan. 2007)..

NOTES:

UNFORGIVENESS

DIRECTIONS ON HOW TO USE THIS MATERIAL

The Unforgiveness, Rejection, and Anger worksheets are to be used together in the following ways:

1. Read and study the material on the stronghold of rejection.

2. Then read and study the material on the stronghold of unforgiveness.

3. Once both of these studies are complete, use the anger worksheet to actually work through the process of granting and receiving forgiveness. The anger worksheet is designed to walk you through the practical steps of addressing those issues you have uncovered by reading and studying the material on rejection and unforgiveness. Do this as your homework assignment for this week.

Ephesians 4:32 (NASB) *And be kind to one another, tenderhearted, forgiving each other, just as God in Christ also has forgiven you.*

One of the most powerful weapons of the enemy against mankind is *unforgiveness*. We live with unhealed wounds as a result of unforgiveness. It produces fruits of bitterness, anger, and rage, and can even lead to murder. It is also an easy way for us to allow the enemy to build strongholds. Unforgiveness lays the foundation for such destructive behavioral patterns as self-protection and self-preservation.

The opposite of unforgiveness is forgiveness. Forgiveness is the very foundation of God's kingdom and the very nature of God Himself. Loosed from the bondage that unforgiveness brings, we can begin to heal and the very love of God can begin to flow through us to others.

DIAGNOSING UNFORGIVENESS

❑ I find myself holding grudges.
❑ I retreat into isolation from others.
❑ I erupt in anger, or I boil inside.
❑ I think of ways to get even with others who have hurt me.
❑ I bury the wrongs done to me without really addressing them.
❑ I pity myself.
❑ I carry bitterness and anger against those who have offended me or willfully wronged me.
❑ Instead of stating the truth, I make excuses for those who have hurt or wronged me.
❑ I often feel sorry for myself.
❑ On occasion, I think I'm some kind of martyr.
❑ I feel like nobody has had it as bad as me.
❑ When I get around someone who has hurt me I want to completely ignore them.

❑ I insulate and protect myself behind a wall of defensiveness.

❑ I do not trust others.

❑ I just cannot forgive (usually means I *will not* forgive).

❑ I am angry with God for allowing bad things to happen to me.

❑ I act like nothing happened instead of confronting issues that have hurt me.

How do I know if I have a grudge with a person?

❑ I cannot get over my past. I have fake conversations with them in my head.

❑ I avoid them at all costs, or when I do see them I wish I could hide.

❑ I compare myself to them. I dismiss them.

❑ I am constantly looking for ammunition to gossip about this person's life. They did it to me; now I get to do it to them!

THE KEY TO FORGIVENESS: RELEASING A DEBT

Forgiveness is necessary when we have been violated in one way or another. There is a debt to pay before reconciliation or restoration can take place. The debt might be emotional, relational, financial, or physical; it might be the result of a betrayal, or related to our reputation. Regardless of the situation, a debt is owed to us.

In order to forgive, we must determine that we will pay the debt, and thereby release the offender (or the offending situation) from their obligation to us. *We will not* expect the offender (or the offending situation) to settle the debt: *We* are willing to pay the cost. This is exactly what Jesus did when He released us from having to pay the debt for the sins and violations we commit against Him.

Imagine living with one of your hands tied by a strong cord (the debt against you) to a big wheelbarrow full of sand (violation against you). You have to push that thing around with you everywhere you go. How easy would that be? Yet this is a reasonable picture of the spiritual burden unforgiveness imposes. Forgiving means taking a sword (our willingness to forgive because of the love, grace, mercy, and shed blood of Jesus Christ) and severing that cord, dropping the load of debt, and leaving it behind. What a relief! Entrust yourself, and the offender/offending situation, to God, while you literally cut loose the load of unforgiveness toward the debt and debtor you have been carrying. *You are free!*

SUMMARIZING THE GRACE OF FORGIVENESS

Unforgiveness destroys the person who carries it, and eventually destroys others. Unforgiveness is one of the cornerstones of Satan's kingdom, and it opens the door to a host of other evils.

Forgiveness, on the other hand, streams from God's own heart. The ability to forgive is based on a love that is not from the world. Jesus often talked about forgiveness with His disciples; He knew it was essential for them, and us, to learn and put into practice. Jesus is our supreme example: He had *every* right and reason to withhold forgiveness, yet instead, He chose to offer it freely.

The Lord's Prayer teaches us to forgive. In Matthew 6:14-15, Jesus said that if we will not forgive others, God will not forgive us. Read that again. The Lord uses some strong language, and there does not appear to be any way around it. Either we forgive others and the Lord forgives us, or we do not forgive others and the Lord does not forgive us! This is a good reason for us to examine our own hearts with great care.

Forgiveness is a choice, not a feeling. Forgiveness does not condone the wrong or hurtful action. Forgiveness grows out of love and flows out of humility (knowing that *we* have hurt others and *we* need forgiveness as well). We are to forgive and release the offender(s) and the offense(s) to God, who alone is the ultimate judge for all of us.

WALKING IN THE TRUST OF FORGIVENESS

Affirm these truth statements out loud in the class:

☑ I will forgive others, just as God has forgiven me.

☑ I will choose to confront issues with forgiveness instead of holding resentment in my heart.

☑ I will offer forgiveness to the perpetrator(s), and leave the rest to God.

☑ I will grow more and more in understanding that the hurts of my past never escaped the eyes of the Lord.

☑ I will not let Satan keep me in the bondage of unforgiveness.

☑ I will forgive others *regardless* of their response to me.

☑ I will allow others to see God's grace, mercy, and forgiveness at work in me!

☑ I know and understand that forgiveness brings freedom and release from my past and present hurts.

SCRIPTURE TO REFLECT UPON

Psalm 25:7 (NLT) *Forgive the rebellious sins of my youth; look instead through the eyes of your unfailing love, for you are merciful, O Lord.*

Psalm 25:11 (NLT) *For the honor of your name, O Lord, forgive my many, many sins.*

Psalm 65:3 (NLT) *Though our hearts are filled with sins, you forgive them all.*

Psalm 79:9 (NLT) *Help us, O God of our salvation! Help us for the honor of Your name. Oh, save us and forgive our sins for the sake of Your name.*

Psalm 103:3 (NLT) *He forgives all my sins and heals all my diseases.*

Psalm 130:4 (NLT) *But you offer forgiveness, that we might learn to fear you.*

Matthew 18:21-35 (NLT) *Then Peter came to Him and asked, "Lord, how often should I forgive someone who sins against me? Seven times?" "No!" Jesus replied. "Seventy times seven! For this reason, the Kingdom of Heaven can be compared to a king who decided to bring his accounts up to date with servants who had borrowed money from him. In the process, one of his debtors was brought in who owed him millions of dollars. He couldn't pay, so the king ordered that he, his wife, his children, and everything he had be sold to pay the debt. But the man fell down before the king and begged him, 'Oh, sir, be patient with me, and I will pay it all.' Then the king was filled with pity for him, and he released him and forgave his debt. But when the man left the king, he went to a fellow servant who owed him a few thousand dollars. He grabbed him by the throat and demanded instant payment. His fellow servant fell down before him and begged for a little more time. 'Be patient and I will pay it,' he pleaded. But his creditor wouldn't wait. He had the man arrested and jailed until the debt could be paid in full. When some of the other servants saw this, they were very upset. They went to the king and told him what had happened. Then the king called in the man he had forgiven and said, 'You evil servant! I forgave you that tremendous debt because you pleaded with me. Shouldn't you have mercy on your fellow servant, just as I had mercy on you?' Then the angry king sent the man to prison until he had paid every penny. That's what my heavenly Father will do to you if you refuse to forgive your brothers and sisters in your heart."*

Mark 11:25-26 (NLT) *"And when you stand praying, if you hold anything against anyone, forgive him, so that your Father in heaven may forgive you your sins."*

Luke 23:32-34 (NLT) *Two other men, both criminals, were also led out with Him to be executed. When they came to the place called the Skull, there they crucified Him, along with the criminals—one on His right, the other on His left. Jesus said, "Father, forgive them, for they do not know what they are doing." And they divided up His clothes by casting lots.*

Ephesians 1:7 (NLT) *In him we have redemption through his blood, the forgiveness of sins, in accordance with the riches of God's grace.*

Ephesians 2:4-5 (NLT) *But God is so rich in mercy, and He loved us so very much, that even while we were dead because of our sins, He gave us life when He raised Christ from the dead. (It is only by God's special favor that you have been saved!)*

Ephesians 4:32 (NLT) *Be kind and compassionate to one another, forgiving each other, just as in Christ God forgave you.*

Colossians 3:13 (NLT) *You must make allowance for each other's faults and forgive the person who offends you. Remember, the Lord forgave you, so you must forgive others.*

James 2:13 (NLT) *For there will be no mercy for you if you have not been merciful to others. But if you have been merciful, then God's mercy toward you will win out over his judgment against you.*

1 John 1:9 (NLT) *If we confess our sins, He is faithful and just and will forgive us our sins and purify us from all unrighteousness.*

DO NOT FORGET THESE:

We must conduct a serious campaign against unforgiveness. The following "4-R's" will help guide you. *You must:*

☑ **REPENT** of the sin of unforgiveness. Confess (be specific) any and all attitudes and actions of living with unforgiveness and unhealed wounds.

☑ **RECEIVE** the Lord's forgiveness for this sin. Receive the infilling and empowering work of the Holy Spirit to walk as Christ did. We must at all times depend on and receive that work in faith.

☑ **REBUKE** the enemy's influence surrounding unhealed wounds and renounce his lies causing you to hang onto unforgiveness. Grant forgiveness and blessing wherever necessary.

☑ **REPLACE** unforgiveness with a spirit of forgiveness by continually renewing your mind in Christ's law.

CORRIE TEN BOOM ON FORGIVENESS

Corrie Ten Boom and her beloved sister were prisoners in Ravensbruck, where they saw, and were subjected to, the atrocities of the Holocaust. The following episode occurred shortly after the end of World War II and Corrie's release from the concentration camp. It is a courageous account of forgiveness!

It was in a church in Munich that I saw him—a balding, heavy-set man in a gray overcoat, a brown felt hat clutched between his hands. People were filing out of the basement room where I had just spoken, moving along the rows of wooden chairs to the door at the rear. It was 1947, and I had come from Holland to defeated Germany with the message that God forgives.

The solemn faces stared back at me, not quite daring to believe. There were never questions after a talk in Germany in 1947. People stood up in silence, in silence collected their wraps, in silence left the room.

And that's when I saw him working his way forward against the others. One moment I saw the overcoat and the brown hat; the next, a blue uniform and a visored cap with its skull and crossbones. It came back with a rush: that huge room with its hard overhead lights; the pathetic pile of dresses and shoes in the center of the floor; the shame of walking naked past this man. I could see my sister's frail form ahead of me, ribs sharp beneath the parchment of skin. Betsie, how thin you were!

The place was Ravensbruck, and the man who was making his way forward had been a guard—one of the most cruel guards. I would recognize him anywhere.

Now he was in front of me, hand thrust out: "A fine message, Fraulein! How good it is to know that, as you say, all our sins are at the bottom of the sea!"

Now I, who had spoken so glibly of forgiveness, fumbled in my pocketbook, rather than take that hand. He could not remember me of course—how could he remember one prisoner among those thousands of women? But I remembered him, and the leather crop swinging from his belt. I was face to face with one of my captors, and my blood seemed to freeze.

"You mentioned Ravensbruck in your talk," he was saying. "I was a guard there." No, he did not remember me.

"But since that time I became a Christian. I know that God has forgiven me for the cruel things I did there, but I would like to hear it from your lips as well. Fraulein" – again the hand came out –"will you forgive me?"

I stood there—I, whose sins had again and again needed to be forgiven—and I could not forgive. Betsie had died in that place—could he erase her slow, terrible death simply for the asking?

It could not have been many seconds that he stood there —hand held out—but to me it seemed hours as I wrestled with the most difficult thing I had ever had to do.

For I had to do it—I knew that. The message was that God forgives those who have injured us. I knew it not only as a commandment of God, but as a daily experience.

Since the end of the war I had a home in Holland for the victims of Nazi brutality. Those who were able to forgive their former enemies were able also to return to the outside world and rebuild their lives, no matter what the physical scars. Those who nursed their bitterness remained invalids. It was as simple and as horrible as that.

And still I stood there with the coldness clutching my heart. But forgiveness is not an emotion—I knew that too.

Forgiveness is an act of the will, and the will can function regardless of the temperature of the heart. "Jesus, help me!" I prayed silently. "I can lift my hand. I can do that much. You supply the feeling."

And so woodenly, mechanically, I thrust my hand into the one stretched out to me. And as I did, an incredible thing took place. The current started in my shoulder, raced down my arm and sprang into our joined hands. And then this healing warmth seemed to flood my whole being, bringing tears to my eyes.

"I forgive you, brother!" I cried. "With all my heart."

For a moment we grasped each others' hands—the former guard and the former prisoner. I had never known God's love so intensely as I did then. But even so, I realized it was not my love. I had tried, and did not have the power. It was the power of the Holy Spirit transforming me in God's love.

"I'm still Learning to Forgive," by Corrie Ten Boom is reprinted with permission from *Guideposts* magazine. Copyright © 1972 by Guideposts, Carmel, New York 10512. All rights reserved.

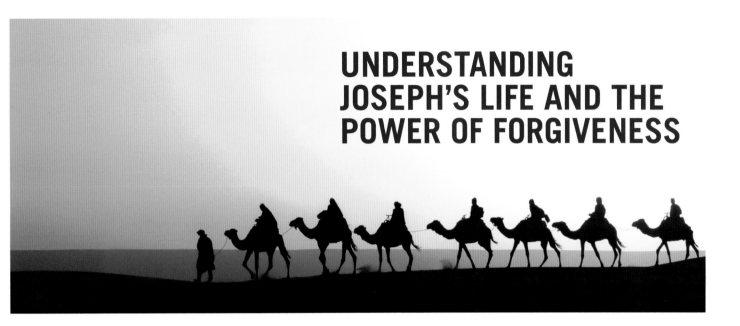

UNDERSTANDING JOSEPH'S LIFE AND THE POWER OF FORGIVENESS

Joseph's life is a classic example of the power of forgiveness and unforgiveness. The story begins with the birth of Joseph, son of Jacob and his wife Rachel. Joseph had a big problem: Even though he was the youngest of eleven brothers, he was his father's favorite, *"because he was the son of his old age"* (Genesis 37:3).

Unfortunately for Joseph, his father Jacob did not conceal the fact that Joseph was his favorite. Jacob made a very beautiful and special coat for Joseph. It was a garment of honor, something usually given only to the firstborn son. When the coat was presented to Joseph, his half-brothers began to hate him.

Joseph also had dreams. In his youthful indiscretion and pride, he readily shared the dreams with his brothers. There was only one problem: the dreams portrayed the brothers being subordinate to Joseph, and bowing down before him! The brothers' hearts were filled with unforgiveness and hatred, not only toward Joseph, but also toward their father Jacob, and they began to think of ways to get rid of the younger and favored brother.

Jacob sent the brothers to find new pasture for the family flocks. After they had been away for some time, he sent Joseph with provisions for them. Unforgiveness and bitterness had now had several years to develop and were about to produce their evil fruit.

Genesis 37:18-20 (NIV) *When Joseph's brothers saw him coming, they recognized him in the distance and made plans to kill him. "Here comes that dreamer!" they exclaimed. "Come on, let's kill him and throw him into a deep pit. We can tell our father that a wild animal has eaten him. Then we'll see what becomes of all his dreams!"*

Joseph arrived in their camp with provisions from home. He was happy and excited to see his brothers, and he could not expect that they would take action against him in a way that would change his life forever. Joseph's brothers threw him into the pit, but his brother Reuben convinced them to spare Joseph's life, which they did. When they spotted a band of Ishmaelite traders, they pulled Joseph out of the pit, removed his robe, and sold him to the traders for twenty pieces of silver. Off to Egypt went Joseph, as a slave.

The story gets uglier. The brothers took Joseph's coat, soaked it in blood, and tore it to shreds to make it appear that a wild animal had attacked Joseph. The brothers took the coat back to their father and lied to him, saying that Joseph had been killed. Imagine Jacob's grief! Worse yet, and more to the point, imagine the unforgiveness and bitterness which caused Joseph's own brothers to even contemplate killing him. Even when they saw the grief of their father, the brothers showed no remorse, nor did they express any concern for their little brother.

So what about Joseph? He was torn from his family, his land, and everything familiar to him. He was bound and tied behind the camels, wondering what he had done to deserve this treatment, thinking of his father's sorrow, and not knowing if he would live or die.

Joseph was sold on the slave block to Potiphar, Pharaoh's officer (as a house slave). Joseph found favor in Potiphar's house and eventually became head slave over his household. However, Potiphar's wife unjustly accused Joseph of rape so he was thrown into prison even though he was innocent.

If anyone had reasons for *unforgiveness*, it was Joseph. He had every "right" to be bitter and angry, filled with rage, self-pity, resentment, etc.

Genesis 39:21-23 (NIV) *But the Lord was with Joseph there, too, and He granted Joseph favor with the chief jailer. Before long, the jailer put Joseph in charge of all the other prisoners, and over everything that happened in the prison. The chief jailer had no more worries after that, because Joseph took care of everything. The Lord was with him, making everything run smoothly and successfully.*

The Lord was there all along; He had not abandoned Joseph. But why did God let all those things happen to Joseph? God had a plan to build a man and save a nation. The things committed against Joseph were real; they hurt, they pierced his heart. Yet Joseph's story ends with him as second in command in Egypt, and with his brothers bowing down before him.

Joseph may have been in prison, but he was not in the self-imposed prison of unforgiveness! Because of a famine in the land, his brothers and family were in need, and came to Egypt seeking assistance. They came to the governor of the land, Joseph. His brothers did not recognize him, but he provided them with a great dinner and treated them kindly—not once, but twice. When he could stand it no longer, he told them who he was:

Genesis 45:1-8 (NIV) *Then Joseph could not control himself before all those who stood by him, and he cried, "Have everyone go out from me." So there was no man with him when Joseph made himself known to his brothers. He wept*

so loudly that the Egyptians heard it, and the household of Pharaoh heard of it. Then Joseph said to his brothers, "I am Joseph! Is my father still alive?" But his brothers could not answer him, for they were dismayed at his presence. Then Joseph said to his brothers, "Please come closer to me." And they came closer. And he said, "I am your brother Joseph, whom you sold into Egypt. Now do not be grieved or angry with yourselves, because you sold me here, for God sent me before you to preserve life. For the famine has been in the land these two years, and there are still five years in which there will be neither plowing nor harvesting. God sent me before you to preserve for you a remnant in the earth, and to keep you alive by a great deliverance. Now, therefore, it was not you who sent me here, but God; and He has made me a father to Pharaoh and lord of all his household and ruler over all the land of Egypt."

Joseph had come to understand that God was aware of his trials, had a purpose for them, and would use all that he had gone through. How about you? Do you see and understand that God is aware of and understands all you go through? That understanding was an essential ingredient in Joseph's ability to choose to forgive!

APPLICATION:

Immediate prayer time within the class:
Declare as a class who you are in Christ! Come against every lie that you are rejected, abandoned, and forgotten. Give to the Lord every false comfort that comes to mind. Begin the process of releasing every bit of unforgiveness that has come from being rejected by others.

Take time this week to sincerely forgive every person who has rejected you or who you feel unforgiveness toward because of what they have done. Be released! Release them! Be free! If you need to ask forgiveness because of your actions, step out and do it with the Lord's leading.

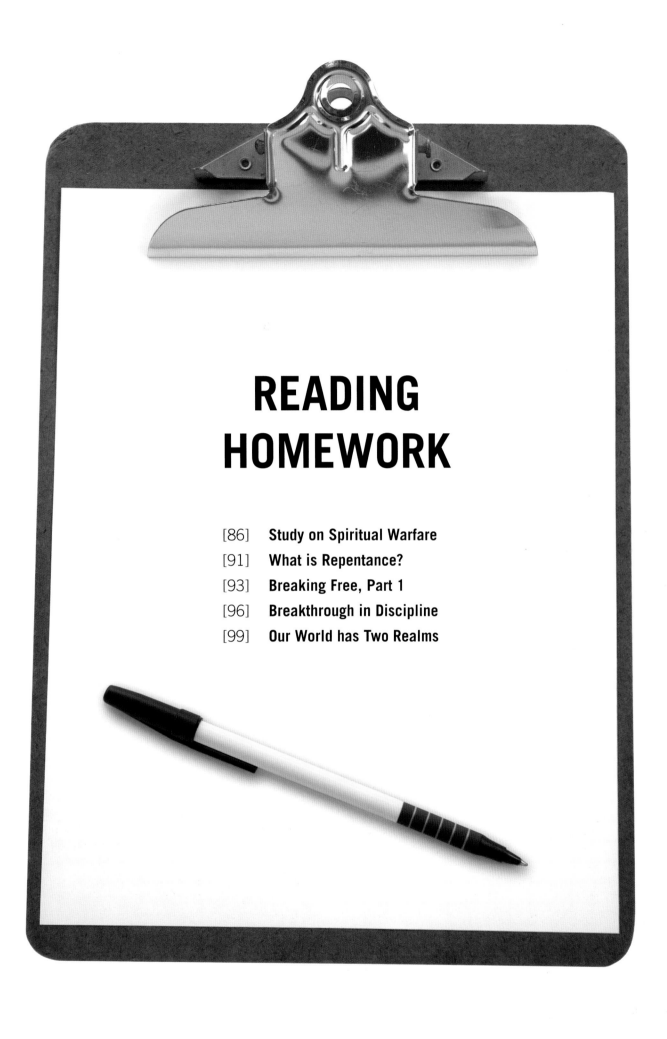

READING HOMEWORK

[86]   **Study on Spiritual Warfare**

[91]   **What is Repentance?**

[93]   **Breaking Free, Part 1**

[96]   **Breakthrough in Discipline**

[99]   **Our World has Two Realms**

[1] STUDY ON SPIRITUAL WARFARE

All Scripture in this section is New International Version.

EVERY CHILD OF GOD HAS BEEN GIVEN A PROMISE OF VICTORY OVER SATAN

Isaiah 54:17 *"No weapon forged against you will prevail, and you will refute every tongue that accuses you. This is the heritage of the servants of the LORD, and this is their vindication from me," declares the LORD.*

Malachi 4:3 *"Then you will trample down the wicked; they will be ashes under the soles of your feet on the day when I do these things," says the LORD Almighty.*

Luke 10:19 *I have given you authority to trample on snakes and scorpions and to overcome all the power of the enemy; nothing will harm you.*

Romans 8:38-39 *For I am convinced that neither death nor life, neither angels nor demons, neither the present nor the future, nor any powers, neither height nor depth, nor anything else in all creation, will be able to separate us from the love of God that is in Christ Jesus our Lord.*

James 4:7 *Submit yourselves, then, to God. Resist the devil, and he will flee from you.*

1 John 4:4 *You, dear children, are from God and have overcome them, because the one who is in you is greater than the one who is in the world.*

IT IS IMPORTANT THAT WE RECOGNIZE WHO OUR ENEMY IS AND WHAT HIS TACTICS ARE

2 Corinthians 2:11 *For we are not unaware of [Satan's] schemes.*

1. **Our battle is not against flesh and blood (things in the natural realm).**

   2 Corinthians 10:3-4 *For though we walk in the flesh, we do not war after the flesh. For the weapons of our warfare are not carnal . . .*

   2 Corinthians 10:3-5 *For though we live in the world, we do not wage war as the world does. The weapons we fight with are not the weapons of the world. On the contrary, they have divine power to demolish strongholds. We demolish arguments and every pretension that sets itself up against the knowledge of God, and we take captive every thought to make it obedient to Christ.*

   Ephesians 6:12 *For our struggle is not against flesh and blood, but against the rulers, against the authorities, against the powers of this dark world and against the spiritual forces of evil in the heavenly realms.*

2. **Authority must be taken over Satan's attempts to hinder the work and the Word of God.** There are spiritual powers that must be broken.

   Daniel 10:12-13 *Then he continued, "Do not be afraid, Daniel. Since the first day that you set your mind to gain understanding and to humble yourself before your God, your words were heard, and I have come in response to them. But the prince of the Persian kingdom resisted me twenty-one days. Then Michael, one of the chief princes, came to help me, because I was detained there with the king of Persia.*

   1 Thessalonians 2:18 *For we wanted to come to you—certainly I, Paul, did, again and again—but Satan stopped us.*

3. **Satan's main device is deception.**

   a. **Subtlety.**

      Genesis 3:1 *Now the serpent was more crafty than any of the wild animals the LORD God had made. He said to the woman, "Did God really say, 'You must not eat from any tree in the garden'?"*

      2 Corinthians 11:3 *But I am afraid that just as Eve was deceived by the serpent's cunning, your minds may somehow be led astray from your sincere and pure devotion to Christ.*

   b. **Doubt.**

      Luke 4:3 *The devil said to him, "If you are the Son of God, tell this stone to become bread."*

      Luke 4:9 *The devil led him to Jerusalem and had him stand on the highest point of the temple. "If you are the Son of God," he said, "throw yourself down from here."*

Matthew 4:6 *"If you are the Son of God," he said, "throw yourself down. For it is written: 'He will command his angels concerning you, and they will lift you up in their hands, so that you will not strike your foot against a stone.'"*

c. **Lies.**

Genesis 3:4 *"You will not surely die," the serpent said to the woman.*

John 8:44 *You belong to your father, the devil, and you want to carry out your father's desire. He was a murderer from the beginning, not holding to the truth, for there is no truth in him. When he lies, he speaks his native language, for he is a liar and the father of lies.*

THE BIBLE USES SEVERAL METAPHORS TO DESCRIBE THE "FIGHT OF FAITH" THAT THE BELIEVER MUST WAGE AGAINST THE EVIL ONE.

1. **Boxer.**

   1 Corinthians 9:26 *Therefore I do not run like a man running aimlessly; I do not fight like a man beating the air.*

2. **Soldier.**

   2 Timothy 2:3-5 *Endure hardship with us like a good soldier of Christ Jesus. No one serving as a soldier gets involved in civilian affairs—he wants to please his commanding officer. Similarly, if anyone competes as an athlete, he does not receive the victor's crown unless he competes according to the rules.*

   Ephesians 6:11-17 *Put on the full armor of God so that you can take your stand against the devil's schemes. For our struggle is not against flesh and blood, but against the rulers, against the authorities, against the powers of this dark world and against the spiritual forces of evil in the heavenly realms. Therefore put on the full armor of God, so that when the day of evil comes, you may be able to stand your ground, and after you have done everything, to stand. Stand firm then, with the belt of truth buckled around your waist, with the breastplate of righteousness in place, and with your feet fitted with the readiness that comes from the gospel of peace. In addition to all this, take up the shield of faith, with which you can extinguish all the flaming arrows of the evil one. Take the helmet of salvation and the sword of the Spirit, which is the word of God.*

3. **Wrestler.**

   Ephesians 6:12 *For our struggle is not against flesh and blood, but against the rulers, against the authorities, against the powers of this dark world and against the spiritual forces of evil in the heavenly realms.*

WHAT DOES IT MEAN TO RESIST THE DEVIL? HOW IS THIS DONE?

1. **Put on the full armor of God.**

   a. **Truth.**

      Ephesians 6:14 *Stand firm then, with the belt of truth buckled around your waist, with the breastplate of righteousness in place . . .*

   b. **Righteousness.**

   c. **Salvation.**

      Ephesians 6:17 *. . . and take the helmet of salvation and the sword of the Spirit, which is the word of God.*

      1 Thessalonians 5:8 *But since we belong to the day, let us be self-controlled, putting on faith and love as a breastplate, and the hope of salvation as a helmet.*

   d. **The Gospel of Peace.**

      Ephesians 6:15 *. . . and with your feet fitted with the readiness that comes from the gospel of peace.*

   e. **Faith.**

      1 Thessalonians 5:8 *But since we belong to the day, let us be self-controlled, putting on faith and love as a breastplate, and the hope of salvation as a helmet.*

      i. Paul says that faith is of primary importance: "above all."

         Ephesians 6:16 *In addition to all this, take up the shield of faith, with which you can extinguish all the flaming arrows of the evil one.*

         1 Peter 5:8-9 *Be self-controlled and alert. Your enemy the devil prowls around like a roaring lion looking for someone to devour. Resist him, standing firm in the faith, because you know that your brothers throughout the world are undergoing the same kind of sufferings.*

1 John 5:4-5 *For everyone born of God overcomes the world. This is the victory that has overcome the world, even our faith. Who is it that overcomes the world? Only he who believes that Jesus is the Son of God.*

ii. But faith and the word are inseparable.

    A. The word did not profit them if not mixed with faith.

    Hebrews 4:2 *For we also have had the gospel preached to us, just as they did; but the message they heard was of no value to them, because those who heard did not combine it with faith.*

    B. Yet faith comes through the word (look up the word "rhema") of God.

    Romans 10:17 *Consequently, faith comes from hearing the message, and the message is heard through the word of Christ.*

    C. It must be both by confession of the mouth and belief in the heart.

    Romans 10:9 *That if you confess with your mouth, "Jesus is Lord," and believe in your heart that God raised him from the dead, you will be saved.*

f. The word of God.

Ephesians 6:17 *Take the helmet of salvation and the sword of the Spirit, which is the word of God.*

Mark 11:24-25 *Therefore I tell you, whatever you ask for in prayer, believe that you have received it, and it will be yours. And when you stand praying, if you hold anything against anyone, forgive him, so that your Father in heaven may forgive you your sins."*

Numbers 13:30 *Then Caleb silenced the people before Moses and said, "We should go up and take possession of the land, for we can certainly do it."*

i. It was the spoken word that Jesus used in confronting the devil in the wilderness. He did not recite miscellaneous scriptures to the devil, but delivered the word of God with authority and power.

    Luke 4:4 *Jesus answered, "It is written: 'Man does not live on bread alone.'"*

Luke 4:10 *For it is written: "He will command his angels concerning you to guard you carefully;"*

Luke 4:12 *Jesus answered, "It says: 'Do not put the Lord your God to the test.'"*

ii. Notice that this is the only offensive part of the armor, referred to in Scripture as a "two-edged sword."

Psalm 149:6-9 *May the praise of God be in their mouths and a double-edged sword in their hands, to inflict vengeance on the nations and punishment on the peoples, to bind their kings with fetters, their nobles with shackles of iron, to carry out the sentence written against them. This is the glory of all his saints. Praise the* Lord*!*

Ephesians 6:17 *Take the helmet of salvation and the sword of the Spirit, which is the word of God.*

Hebrews 4:12 *For the word of God is living and active. Sharper than any double-edged sword, it penetrates even to dividing soul and spirit, joints and marrow; it judges the thoughts and attitudes of the heart.*

Revelations 2:16 *Repent therefore! Otherwise, I will soon come to you and will fight against them with the sword of my mouth.*

2. The weapon of praise.

Numbers 10:9 *When you go into battle in your own land against an enemy who is oppressing you, sound a blast on the trumpets. Then you will be remembered by the LORD your God and rescued from your enemies.*

Numbers 10:35 *Whenever the ark set out, Moses said, "Rise up, O LORD! May your enemies be scattered; May your foes flee before you."*

Numbers 31:6-7 *Moses sent them into battle, a thousand from each tribe, along with Phinehas son of Eleazar, the priest, who took with him articles from the sanctuary and the trumpets for signaling. They fought against Midian, as the LORD commanded Moses, and killed every man.*

1 Samuel 16:23 *Whenever the spirit from God came upon Saul, David would take his harp and play. Then relief would come to Saul; he would feel better, and the evil spirit would leave him.*

2 Chronicles 20:21-22 *After consulting the people, Jehoshaphat appointed men to sing to the LORD and to praise him for the splendor of his holiness as they went out at the head of the army, saying: "Give thanks to the LORD, for his love endures forever." As they began to sing and praise, the LORD set ambushes against the men of Ammon and Moab and Mount Seir who were invading Judah, and they were defeated.*
(Note especially the fact that it was their initiative: "when they began . . .")

Psalm 68:1-2 *May God arise, may his enemies be scattered; may his foes flee before him. As smoke is blown away by the wind, may you blow them away; As wax melts before the fire, may the wicked perish before God.*

Psalm 149:5-9 (see previous page)

Isaiah 33:3 *At the thunder of your voice, the peoples flee; when you rise up, the nations scatter.*

Acts 16:24-26 *Upon receiving such orders, he put them in the inner cell and fastened their feet in the stocks. About midnight Paul and Silas were praying and singing hymns to God, and the other prisoners were listening to them. Suddenly there was such a violent earthquake that the foundations of the prison were shaken. At once all the prison doors flew open, and everybody's chains came loose.*

3. The anointing.

1 Samuel 16:14-23 *Now the Spirit of the LORD had departed from Saul, and an evil spirit from the LORD tormented him. Saul's attendants said to him, "See, an evil spirit from God is tormenting you. Let our lord command his servants here to search for someone who can play the harp. He will play when the evil spirit from God comes upon you, and you will feel better."*

So Saul said to his attendants, "Find someone who plays well and bring him to me."

One of the servants answered, "I have seen a son of Jesse of Bethlehem who knows how to play the harp. He is a brave man and a warrior. He speaks well and is a fine-looking man. And the LORD is with him."

Then Saul sent messengers to Jesse and said, "Send me your son David, who is with the sheep." So Jesse took a donkey loaded with bread, a skin of wine and a young goat and sent them with his son David to Saul.

David came to Saul and entered his service. Saul liked him very much, and David became one of his armor-bearers. Then Saul sent word to Jesse, saying, "Allow David to remain in my service, for I am pleased with him."

Whenever the spirit from God came upon Saul, David would take his harp and play. Then relief would come to Saul; he would feel better, and the evil spirit would leave him.

Isaiah 10:27 *In that day their burden will be lifted from your shoulders, their yoke from your neck; the yoke will be broken because you have grown so fat.*

4. Prayer.

Luke 22:31-32 *"Simon, Simon, Satan has asked to sift you as wheat. But I have prayed for you, Simon, that your faith may not fail. And when you have turned back, strengthen your brothers."*

TO STAND VICTORIOUSLY IN BATTLE AGAINST THE ENEMY, CERTAIN SPIRITUAL REQUIREMENTS MUST BE MET IN THE LIFE OF THE BELIEVER.

1. Obedience.

Deuteronomy 11:22-25 *If you carefully observe all these commands I am giving you to follow—to love the LORD your God, to walk in all his ways and to hold fast to him—then the LORD will drive out all these nations before you, and you will dispossess nations larger and stronger than you. Every place where you set your foot will be yours: Your territory will extend from the desert to Lebanon, and from the Euphrates River to the western sea. No man will be able to stand against you. The LORD your God, as he promised you, will put the terror and fear of you on the whole land, wherever you go.*

Deuteronomy 28:1 *If you fully obey the LORD your God and carefully follow all his commands I give you today, the LORD your God will set you high above all the nations on earth.*

Deuteronomy 28:7 *The LORD will grant that the enemies who rise up against you will be defeated before you. They will come at you from one direction but flee from you in seven.*

2. A right relationship with God.

Deuteronomy 11:22-25 (See above)

Psalm 91 *He who dwells in the shelter of the Most High will rest in the shadow of the Almighty. I will say of the L*ORD*, "He is my refuge and my fortress, my God, in whom I trust." Surely he will save you from the fowler's snare and from the deadly pestilence. He will cover you with his feathers, and under his wings you will find refuge; his faithfulness will be your shield and rampart. You will not fear the terror of night, nor the arrow that flies by day, nor the pestilence that stalks in the darkness, nor the plague that destroys at midday. A thousand may fall at your side, ten thousand at your right hand, but it will not come near you. You will only observe with your eyes and see the punishment of the wicked. If you make the Most High your dwelling— even the LORD, who is my refuge— then no harm will befall you, no disaster will come near your tent. For he will command his angels concerning you to guard you in all your ways; They will lift you up in their hands, so that you will not strike your foot against a stone. You will tread upon the lion and the cobra; you will trample the great lion and the serpent. "Because he loves me," says the LORD, "I will rescue him; I will protect him, for he acknowledges my name. He will call upon me, and I will answer him; I will be with him in trouble, I will deliver him and honor him. With long life will I satisfy him and show him my salvation."*

3. Give the devil no foothold

Ephesians 4:27 *. . . and do not give the devil a foothold.*

It is the responsibility of the believer to prepare for battle, to put on the whole armor of god" (Ephesians 6:11), and to "stand against the evil one" (v. 11-14). These are active verbs. But it is God who fights the battle. Indeed, Jesus Christ has already defeated the enemy for us. We must simply walk in the victory!

Deuteronomy 20:1 *When you go to war against your enemies and see horses and chariots and an army greater than yours, do not be afraid of them, because the LORD your God, who brought you up out of Egypt, will be with you.*

2 Chronicles 20:15 *He said: "Listen, King Jehoshaphat and all who live in Judah and Jerusalem! This is what the LORD says to you: 'Do not be afraid or discouraged because of this vast army. For the battle is not yours, but God's.*

Colossians 2:15 *And having disarmed the powers and authorities, he made a public spectacle of them, triumphing over them by the cross.*

NOTES:

[2] WHAT IS REPENTANCE?
By Catherine Booth

If any father has a prodigal son, I ask, how is it that you are reconciled to your son? You love him intensely. Probably you are more conscious of your love for him than for any other of your children. Your heart yearns over him, you pray for him, you dream of him, your bowels yearn over him. Why are you not reconciled? Why are you obligated to hold him at arm's length and not have him come in and out, and live with you on the same terms as the affectionate, obedient daughter? "Oh!" you say, "the case is different, I cannot. It is not, I would not, but I cannot." "Before that can possibly be, the boy's feeling must be changed toward me. I have done all a father could do, but he will go on in defiance of my will." You say, "As a wise and righteous father I must insist on a change in him. He must confess his sin and ask me to forgive him. Then I should run to meet him and put my arms around his neck!" But there is a "cannot" in the case.

Just so. It is not that God does not love you, sinner, or that the great benevolent heart of God has not, as it were, wept tears of blood over you. It is not that He would not put His loving arms around you this moment if you would only come to His feet, and confess your wrong, and seek His pardon. He cannot. The laws of His universe are against His doing so. He dare not and cannot until there is a change of mind in you. You must repent, "Except ye repent, ye shall all likewise perish."

Well, if repentance be an indispensable condition of salvation, let us try to find out what repentance really is. How full of confusion the world and the Church are upon this subject! Repentance is not merely conviction of sin. If it were, what a different world we should have, for there are tens of thousands in whose hearts God's Spirit has done His work of convincing them of sin. We should be perfectly astounded if we had any conception of the multitude whom God has convinced of sin, as he did Agrippa and Festus. They are convinced of sin, but they go no further. They live this week as they did last. That is not repentance.

Neither is repentance mere sorrow for sin. I have seen people weep bitterly and writhe and struggle, yet hug their idols, and vain has it been to try to shake these from them. If Jesus Christ would have saved them with those idols, they would have had no objection at all. If they could have got through the strait gate with one particular idol, they would have gone through long since, but to part with it is another thing. Some people will weep like your stubborn child when you want him to do something which he does not want to do. He will cry, and when you apply the rod he will cry harder, but he will not yield. When he yields he becomes a penitent, but until he does he is merely a convicted sinner.

When God applies the rod of His Spirit, of His providence, and His word, sinners will cry, wince, and whine and make you believe they are praying and want to be saved, but all the while they are holding their necks as stiff as iron. They will not submit. The moment they submit they become true penitents and are saved. There is no mistake more common than for people to suppose they are repentant when they are not. Repentance, therefore, is not mere sorrow for sin. A man may be ever so sorry and all the way down to death be hugging some forbidden thing, as the young ruler hugged his possessions. But that is not repentance. Neither is repentance a promise that you will forsake sin in the future. If it were, there would be many more penitents. There is scarcely a poor drunkard that does not promise, in his own mind, or to his poor wife, or somebody, that he will forsake his cups. There is scarcely any kind of a sinner who does not continually promise that he will one day give up his sin and turn to God, but he does not do it.

What then is repentance? Repentance is simply renouncing sin, turning round from darkness to light, from the power of Satan unto God. This is giving up sin in your heart, in purpose, in desire; resolving that you will give up every evil thing, and that you will do it now. Of course this involves sorrow; for how will any sane man turn himself round from a given course into another if he does not repent? It implies, also, hatred of the course he formerly took, and from which he turns.

He is like the prodigal who, when he sat in the swine yard amongst the husks and the filth, fully resolved, and at last acted. He went, and that was the test of his repentance. He might have sat resolving and promising till now, if he had lived as long, and he would never have got the father's kiss, the father's welcome, if he had not started. Yet, he went, and went to his father honestly and said, "I have sinned" which implied a great deal more in his language then than it does in ours now. Then comes the proof of his submission, "and am no more worthy to be called thy son: make me as one of thy hired servants"—put me in a stable, or set me to clean the boots, so that I can be in thy family and have thy smile. That is Jesus Christ's own beautiful illustration of true repentance. Submission is the test of true repentance. My child may be willing to do a hundred and fifty other things, but if he is not willing to submit on the one point of controversy he is a rebel and remains one until he yields.

Here is the difference between a spurious and a real repentance. I am afraid we have had, in our churches thousands who had a spurious repentance: they were convinced of sin—they were sorry for it; they wanted to live a better life, to love God in a sort of general way; but they skipped over the real point of controversy with God; they hid it from their pastor, perhaps, and from the deacons, and from the people who talked with them. Abraham might have been willing to give up every other thing he possessed, but if he had not been willing to give up Isaac, all else would have been useless. It is your Isaac that God wants. You have an Isaac, just as the young ruler had his possessions. You have something that you are holding on to, that the Holy Spirit says you must let go, and you say, "I can't." Very well, then you must you must stop outside the Kingdom.

Then another difficulty comes in, and people say, "I have not the power to repent." There is a grand mistake. You have the power, or God would not command it. You can repent!

You can this moment lift up your eyes to Heaven and say, with the prodigal, "Father, I have sinned, and I renounce my sin." You may not be able to weep. God nowhere requires or commands that. You are able, this very moment, to renounce sin in purpose and in resolution. Mind you do not confound the renouncing of the sin with the power of saving yourself from it. If you renounce it, Jesus will come and save you from it, like the man with the withered hand whom Jesus intended to heal. Where was the power to come from to heal him? From Jesus, the benevolence, the love, that prompted that healing all came from Jesus; but Jesus wanted a condition, and that was the response of the man's will. So He said, "Stretch forth thine hand." If the man had been like some of you he would have said, "What an unreasonable command! You know I cannot do it." Jesus wanted that "I will, Lord" to be inside the man, the response of his will. The moment he said that, Jesus supplied strength. He stretched forth his hand and you know what happened.

Stretch out your withered hand, whatever it may be, and say, "I will, Lord." You have the power and mind, you have the obligation, which is universal and immediate. God "now commandeth all men every where to repent" and to believe the gospel. What a tyrant He must be if He commands that and yet knows you have not the power!

Now, do not say, "I do not feel enough." Do you feel enough to be willing to forsake your sin? That is the point. Any man who does not repent enough to forsake his sin is not a penitent at all. When you repent enough to forsake your sin, that moment your repentance is sincere and you may take hold of Jesus with a firm grasp. Then "believe on the Lord Jesus Christ, and thou shalt be saved."

Catherine Booth was born in 1829 and married William Booth in 1855. They began the Christian Mission, which later became the Salvation Army, in London's East End in 1864, where she preached often. She died in 1890 after leading a charge to improve the working conditions of women and children, equalizing their wages and conditions with men at the time.

[3] BREAKING FREE, PART 1
By Mike Riches (excerpts from his book *One World-Two Realms: Operating in Christ's Authority***)**

INTRODUCTION TO AUTHORITY

When our Christian lives are lived according to God's design, more than our natural capacity is required. We need God's supernatural power on every front. It Is His radical power that gives us the strength to live set apart and distinct in this world. We need this power to live out the ministry and mission Jesus left us on earth to do. It is based on the supernatural authority given to us through Jesus Christ. It moves far beyond mere theological jargon: It is the reality of Christ in real-life application.

The supernatural authority and power of Jesus Christ is yours. He wants you to understand it; He wants you to use it. His authority is a gift to us, yet most of us are inexperienced in its practice. Some are even totally unaware of this amazing resource. Many are also unfamiliar with the lifestyle of the Church in the New Testament era described in the book of Acts. Consequently, we fall far short of God's design for our lives and the Church.

OUR NEED TO UNDERSTAND AND APPROPRIATE GOD'S POWER

Most of us (as believing followers of Jesus Christ) agree that we are in desperate need of understanding God's supernatural power that is at work within us and around us. We need desperately to understand our true identity in Christ and how He wants to use us. Paul thought this as well, for this was Paul's prayer for all true followers of Christ:

Ephesians 1:18-20 (NLT) *I pray that your hearts will be flooded with light so that you can understand the wonderful future He has promised to those He called. I want you to realize what a rich and glorious inheritance He has given to His people. I pray that you will begin to understand the incredible greatness of His power for us who believe Him. This is the same mighty power that raised Christ from the dead and seated Him in the place of honor at God's right hand in the heavenly realms.*

Paul prayed that the eyes of their hearts would be enlightened. He then identified three things he wanted them to realize to greater depth and fullness. First, he prayed they would realize the certain future they have as God's children. Second, he prayed that they would understand their inherited wealth and glory as saints. There is much that could be said on both of these subjects, and it is important to comprehend these truths. For our purposes we will focus on the third subject of Paul's prayer, the "surpassing greatness of His power toward us." It is the same power that resurrected Jesus from death!

Paul recognized the significance of this truth to such a significant degree that it was part of his passionate prayer for God's people. In fact, Paul repeats this prayer throughout the book of Ephesians:

Ephesians 3:19-20 (NLT) *May you experience the love of Christ, though it is so great you will never fully understand it. Then you will be filled with the fullness of life and power that comes from God. Now glory be to God! By His mighty power at work within us, He is able to accomplish infinitely more than we would ever dare to ask or hope.*

In these verses, Paul prays for believers to experience the fullness of Christ's love for them. The New Living Translation translates verse nineteen to say that "then" we will be filled with the fullness of life and power that comes from God.

Paul's prayer is for believers to experience the fullness of God's life and power that "comes from God." We need to note that this is not just any power, but the power that comes from God. Paul had earlier qualified that this is the same power that resurrected Jesus from death. He continues with the exciting news that God's mighty power is at work "within" us!

The power of God in a believer's life was so significant in Paul's mind that when he went to evaluate the authenticity of the "so-called" teachers in Corinth, he evaluated not only their words, but their power.

1 Corinthians 4:19-20 (NASB) *But I will come to you soon, if the Lord wills, and I shall find out, not the words of those who are arrogant, but their power. For the kingdom of God does not consist in words, but in power.*

Jesus also chastised the religious leaders who were trying to trap Him with questions because they did not understand the Scriptures or the power of God:

Mark 12:24 (NLT) *Jesus replied, "Your problem is that you don't know the Scriptures, and you don't know the power of God."*

These are forceful commands, warnings, and exhortations by God through Jesus and the Apostle Paul. We must take heed and commit ourselves to understanding the power of God, its role in His kingdom, and its practical application.

THIS POWER IS IN YOU

Right now is a moment for hands-on learning. Put your hand on your chest. What you need to understand, as a true follower of Jesus Christ, is that the power that resurrected Jesus from death is resident within you! That's right! Within you—at the core of your being, where your hand now resides on your chest—is the death-defying, resurrection power of God.

Ephesians 3:20 (NLT) *Now glory be to God! By His mighty power at work within us, He is able to accomplish infinitely more than we would ever dare to ask or hope.*

This verse goes on to say that this power is given to us for a reason. It is by this power that God will accomplish infinitely more in and through us than we can possibly imagine, or even dare to ask. What would you like God to do in your life for His glory and the advancement of His kingdom? Is it infinitely more than you dare to ask or hope for? His power is given to us for a reason!

Do you ever think about the demonstration of God's mighty power in the Gospels and in the book of Acts? Wow! Peter and John tell the lame man to get up and walk, and he does. In fact, he leaps for joy!

Most of the time we believe we are disqualified from being instruments of God's demonstrated power because we are "normal people." We think that we could never be a Peter, John, or Paul, let alone an Elijah or Moses. But James dashes any potential of "deifying" these men by sharing with us that Elijah was a man, literally just like us.

James 5:17 (NASB) *Elijah was a man with a nature like ours, and he prayed earnestly that it would not rain, and it did not rain on the earth for three years and six months.*

The Scriptures do not hide the foibles of men and women throughout the Biblical accounts. Abraham had his messy days as a human being, as did Moses, King David, and the Apostle Peter. We are not any different. God does not release His power to do strategic and supernatural things in perfect human beings, because there are none! But God does release His power in people whose hearts are humble, hungry, faith-filled and obedient.

It is for this very reason that I love what the Scriptures say about Ananias (not the lying, greedy man, but the one God sent to heal and commission Saul of Tarsus, a persecutor of Christians). As you know, Saul became the Apostle Paul, who was mightily used by God to advance His kingdom during the time of the early Church. And it was an unknown man, Ananias, whom God used to heal Paul's blindness:

Acts 9:10-11 (NKJV) *Now there was a certain disciple at Damascus named Ananias; and to him the Lord said in a vision, "Ananias." And he said, "Here I am, Lord." So the Lord said to him, "Arise and go to the street called Straight, and inquire at the house of Judas for one called Saul of Tarsus, for behold, he is praying.*

Acts 9:17-18 (NKJV) *And Ananias went his way and entered the house; and laying his hands on him he said, "Brother Saul, the Lord Jesus, who appeared to you on the road as you came, has sent me that you may receive your sight and be filled with the Holy Spirit." Immediately there fell from his eyes something like scales, and he received his sight at once; and he arose and was baptized.*

The New King James Version describes Ananias as a "certain disciple." We never hear of him again. We do not read that Ananias had a high position or office in the early church. He was simply a "certain disciple" through whom God exercised His mighty power. I believe I qualify as a "certain disciple," and if you are a believing follower of Jesus Christ you qualify as a "certain disciple" too.

THE CHURCH'S POSITION AND POSTURE

When I use the term "Church," I am not speaking merely of a local church. I refer to all believing followers of Jesus Christ; those who by God's grace, through faith, have received forgiveness of sin, by believing that Jesus died on the cross and resurrected from death to pay for the guilt and debt of sin. Such people make up the Church universal. The local church is the visible expression of the mission of the Church. Therefore, everything stated In regard to the Church is true of each and every local church.

The Church was built to be on the offense. Jesus designed the Church to attack and advance, not to retreat and settle passively for defeat. Too many followers of Jesus Christ are on the defensive. They are passive or backpedal, and wonder when the devil may overpower them. Jesus made it very clear in Matthew 16 that hell is on the defensive, not the church!

Instead of becoming overwhelmed by what Satan does, we need to look at what Christ has done, is doing, and what He has authorized and designed us to do. We are not to be fearful; it is Satan who has the disadvantage! Ours is a place of triumph and authority, not a place of defeat and impotence. Jesus speaks plainly on this point.

Matthew 16:18-19 (NKJV) *"And I also say to you that you are Peter, and on this rock I will build My church, and the gates of Hades shall not prevail against it. And I will give you the keys of the kingdom of heaven, and whatever you bind on earth will be bound in heaven, and whatever you loose on earth will be loosed in heaven." Then He commanded His disciples that they should tell no one that He was Jesus the Christ.*

Let us establish briefly a contextual overview. In this text, Jesus asks the disciples who people say He is. Jesus knew what the people were saying; He had heard. But He was creating a point of instruction with His disciples. When Jesus asks the disciples, "Who do you say that I am?" Peter answers that He is the Messiah, the Son of the Living God. In response, Jesus tells Peter that he is blessed to recognize Him as He truly is. He goes on to say that only God the Father could give Peter that perceptive insight.

ADVANCING AGAINST HELL'S GATES

In the aforementioned text, Jesus said that it was "upon this rock" that Jesus would build His Church. The "rock" is the truth that Jesus is the Messiah. Jesus is the "sent One" of God who is the foundation of His Church. This is strategic in establishing Jesus' authority. He then went on to say that the gates of Hades will not withstand or prevail against His Church. Jesus planned to build His Church. And when you build something; it is formed, developed, grows, and expands. Jesus was clear that the gates of Hades could not restrict or withstand the expansion or growth of the Church of Jesus Christ.

There is a particular insight to explore in these verses. The first piece of insight is connected to the phrase "gates of Hades." In ancient times, it was typical for a city to be surrounded by a fortified wall. The wall was designed to define and protect the city and its inhabitants, and it had several gates. These gates served a few purposes, one of which was to allow citizens, visitors, and merchants to enter and depart the city.

The gates of an ancient city also served as an instrument of protection against enemies and advancing armies. It is important to note that ancient city gates were not offensive weapons; they were defensive instruments. They helped to maintain and secure territory and possessions. A gate never runs into battle!

Gates in an ancient city were a place of business for those in authority. One Biblical example of this is when Boaz conducted official business to gain Ruth's hand in marriage. It was done at the gates of the city (Ruth 4:1). The phrase "gates of the city" is symbolic, and it denotes authority and power. This is similar to when Americans use the phrase, "The White House" when referring to authoritative decision-making in the United States. We know that the physical property of The White House, in Washington, D.C., is incapable of decision-making. However, it represents the men and women who make authoritative decisions that affect the entire country.

The second piece of insight is several important truths that Jesus relayed to His disciples (also in Matthew 16:18-19). First, He declared that the authority and government of Satan's kingdom (gates of Hades) will not withstand the authority, power, and advancement of the Church as it marches in the name of Jesus Christ. Jesus is the ultimate authority, and He has ultimate, infinite power. All the demons of hell, including Satan himself, could simultaneously rise up against Jesus and concentrate every bit of their diabolical power solely to destroy Him; and they would fail miserably. Did they not already try it once? With one word, Jesus could annihilate them instantaneously.

Secondly, He said that the Church should move offensively and aggressively against Satan's kingdom. It is interesting that Jesus said the gates of Hades could not prevail or withstand His building of the Church. We know that gates were shut, barred, and reinforced when an advancing army was coming against a city. The image Jesus gave was that of His Church advancing against the "Prince of the power of the Air," the "Ruler of this world" and his kingdom. As the Church advances to take territory Satan has possessed, the gates of his kingdom cannot withstand the advancing Church of Jesus Christ.

The mission of the Church is to advance and expand. It began with 120 people in an upper room in the small city of Jerusalem, in an insignificant (in the world's eyes) nation called Israel. It advanced to Judea, then Samaria, and then to the ends of the earth. Every person who comes into a redemptive, saving relationship with Jesus Christ is precious plunder seized from Satan by the advancing Church. These people are no longer Satan's possession. Every shattered stronghold, every crushed addiction, every restored marriage, every prodigal who returns, every recovered relationship, every church that is rejuvenated and reformed to God's original design, every healed sickness, every homeless and hungry person that is filled, every advancement of the Gospel constitutes the gates of Hades crumbling under the advancing Church of Jesus Christ! We are to assault and pummel Hades' gates, and we are to advance and take back the territory Satan has stolen from us. He has held back people's lives, families, churches, businesses, and institutions far too long! We are the ambassadors of the reconciling, glorious, liberating Gospel of Jesus Christ!

[4] BREAKTHROUGH IN DISCIPLINE

1 Timothy 4:7 (NKJV) *But reject profane and old wives' fables, and exercise yourself toward godliness.*

1 Timothy 4:7 (NLT) *Do not waste time arguing over godless ideas and old wives' tales. Spend your time and energy in training yourself for spiritual fitness.*

1 Timothy 4:1-16 (MSG) *The Spirit makes it clear that as time goes on, some are going to give up on the faith and chase after demonic illusions put forth by professional liars. These liars have lied so well and for so long that they've lost their capacity for truth. They will tell you not to get married. They'll tell you not to eat this or that food —perfectly good food God created to be eaten heartily and with thanksgiving by Christians! Everything God created is good, and to be received with thanks. Nothing is to be sneered at and thrown out. God's Word and our prayers make every item in creation holy. You've been raised on the Message of the faith and have followed sound teaching. Now pass on this counsel to the Christians there, and you'll be a good servant of Jesus. Stay clear of silly stories that get dressed up as religion. Exercise daily in God—no spiritual flabbiness, please! Workouts in the gymnasium are useful, but a disciplined life in God is far more so, making you fit both today and forever. You can count on this. Take it to heart. This is why we've thrown ourselves into this venture so totally. We're banking on the living God, Savior of all men and women, especially believers. Get the word out. Teach all these things. And don't let anyone put you down because you're young. Teach believers with your life: by word, by demeanor, by love, by faith, by integrity. Stay at your post reading Scripture, giving counsel, teaching. And that special gift of ministry you were given when the leaders of the church laid hands on you and prayed—keep that dusted off and in use. Cultivate these things. Immerse yourself in them. The people will all see you mature right before their eyes! Keep a firm grasp on both your character and your teaching. Don't be diverted. Just keep at it. Both you and those who hear you will experience salvation.*

LOOK AT THE KEY WORDS IN THIS PASSAGE

1. "Refuse" means to decline, shun, reject, beg off, get excused, avoid.

2. "Profane" means lawful to be trodden (hence, profane in the sense of unhallowed, common); the absence of a divine or sacred character.

3. "Fables" means fiction, a fable, an invention, falsehood.

4. "Exercise" (*gumnazo*) speaks of Greek athletes engaging in athletic exercises in a gymnasium. In this usage, the exercise is not that of the physical body but that of the mind, emotions, and will (the spiritual part of a person).

5. "Unto" means "with a view toward." Just as a Greek athlete would exercise with an intent to win in the athletic contest, so Timothy is exhorted to exercise with the intent to excel in godliness.

6. "Godliness" means reverence, respect, and piety toward God.

WHAT COMES TO MIND WHEN YOU THINK OF THE WORD EXERCISE?

1. When was the last time you sweated spiritually?

2. Would you describe your spiritual exercise routine as a regular ten-minute workout or that of a weekend warrior with no exercise during the week?

3. How does a lack of discipline affect what we think about every day?

4. What is the Lord saying to you about discipline?

15 COMMON AREAS IN WHICH WE CAN BECOME LAX IN DISCIPLINE

Take a look at these fifteen areas in which we can grow complacent. Let the accountability begin today as you search your heart!

1. **We are hesitant to *initiate friendships*.**

2. **We fail to *follow up*** (returning calls, schoolwork, finding a job, commitments, etc). We have made verbal commitments to people and organizations, but have failed to follow through.

3. **We have *stopped believing* for certain people.** Remember that love endures and hopes for all things.

1 Corinthians 13:7 (NLT) *Love never gives up, never loses faith, is always hopeful, and endures through every circumstance.*

This means believing for *breakthrough*, for *salvation*, and for *change* for other people. When we give up instead of pressing through and believing, it is like saying, "I'll just wait and see." This is pure passivity.

Believing for people builds endurance. It is easy to believe for two or three days (sometimes for only two or three hours). We are to believe, and there is no set time limit for faith. Jesus said in John 6:29, "This is the work of God, that you believe in Him whom He sent." How long can you believe for others? How long can you believe for yourself?

a. Love does not give up on truth and obedience. Instead, love rejoices with the truth, celebrates obedience, and stands on the promises of God.

b. Love bears all things. How quick are we to cover another person's faults? Love feels the pain of those who fail and helps carry the burden of the hurt.

   Isaiah 53:4-5 (NKJV) *Surely he has borne our griefs and carried our sorrows; yet we esteemed him stricken, smitten by God, and afflicted. But he was wounded for our transgressions, he was bruised for our iniquities; the chastisement for our peace was upon him, and by his stripes we are healed.*

   1 Peter 4:8 (NKJV) *And above all things have fervent love for one another, for "love will cover a multitude of sins."*

c. Love believes all things. Love is not suspicious or cynical. Love always opts for a favorable possibility. Love is not ready to believe the worst about someone.

   Galatians 6:1 (NASB) *Brothers, even if a man is caught in any trespass, you who are spiritual, restore such a one in a spirit of gentleness; each one looking to yourself, so that you too will not be tempted.*

d. Love hopes all things. Even when belief in a loved one's goodness or repentance is shattered, love hopes. When it runs out of faith, it still holds onto hope. As long as God's grace is in play, anything can happen!

4. **We have given up on** *personal revelation* **we have received.** (For example, you know the Lord has spoken to you about aiding a friend in need, but you have ignored His request).

5. **We have neglected to guard our** *minds and mouths.*

6. **We lack the** *physical discipline* **of our body, which is the temple of the Spirit.** (For example, you now know the importance of eating from all major food groups. You cannot be lazy about this and later expect God to fix the problems that come as a result.)

7. **We have been careless about** *spiritual disciplines* (reading the Bible, prayer, intercession, etc.).

8. **We have fled** *trials* **rather than enduring them.** (For example, asking the Lord to change you, but then not receiving the training and equipping opportunities He provided.)

   There may still be sorrow over current trials and character development. We are mourning, complaining, and resisting the Lord in the way He works to change us. We cry out, "Lord, come and change me, rearrange me!" but we don't think about the fact that rearranging us takes work and causes pain.

9. **We have been willing to stop short of** *maturity.* We are not making the choices (daily, hourly, by-the-minute) to put away childish behaviors like arguing with roommates or spouses, looking for excuses, or finding the "easy way out."

10. **We have let distractions draw us away from** *staying focused.* We have given in to the temptation to move away from the goals set before us.

   It is like an individual standing before a target with bow and arrows in hand. Suddenly they begin looking at other nearby targets at which others are shooting, and they start shooting aimlessly at whichever target catches their eye.

   There are four common sources of this lack of discipline:

   a. **Comparison:** "I want to do what they're doing, not what God has asked of me."

   b. **Jealousy:** "I want to be like them, to have what they have (ie. influence), or produce fruit like they do."

   c. **Boredom:** We allow our obedience to God to become mundane and boring for us. This is a lack of mental toughness.

   d. **Relative obedience:** We obey God relatively, not literally, not taking Him at His word. (i.e If He told me to call all five people and I decide to call only three, I am establishing my own plan and "shooting arrows" at my own whim.)

11. **We neglect *praise and thanksgiving.*** We can overlook the importance of expressing our praise and gratitude to God as well as to others.

12. **We choose to hold onto the *injustices* in our life.** This allows us to remain victims and not choose victory. We exaggerate the pain we may have experienced, which is a major distraction from moving forward with other issues; fosters passivity.

13. **We are lacking in our zeal and belief for the *harvest!*** We are like a man throwing out a net but saying, "We won't catch anything anyway."

14. **We need to cultivate our ability and willingness to *wait on God.*** We cannot afford to reject God's timing, modify His process, or challenge His ways. It is like a person constantly checking his or her watch in the middle of a conversation. How rude! The Lord wants to remind us of Noah's enduring patience in waiting to see the fulfillment of his faith – over 100 years!

15. ***We seldom read the Word*** with expectancy. Do we believe whole-heartedly the promises of the Scriptures, even though they seem impossible to the human mind?

    Hebrews 4:12 (NKJV) *For the word of God is living and powerful, and sharper than any two-edged sword, piercing even to the division of soul and spirit, and of joints and marrow, and is a discerner of the thoughts and intents of the heart.*

    Psalm 119:105 (NKJV) *Your word is a lamp to my feet and a light to my path.*

    2 Timothy 3:16-17 (NKJV) *All Scripture is given by inspiration of God, and is profitable for doctrine, for reproof, for correction, for instruction in righteousness, that the man of God may be complete, thoroughly equipped for every good work.*

NOTES:

[5] OUR WORLD HAS TWO REALMS
By Mike Riches (excerpts from his book *One World-Two Realms: Operating in Christ's Authority*)

For years I endured good-natured ribbing from friends because of our television set—they called it a *legend*. Looking back on it now, this "ribbing" was really more like ridicule! About twenty years earlier my wife and I received it as a second-hand TV. It was a monstrous console TV set that could have easily served as an anchor for virtually any sea-worthy vessel. You know the type; it looked more like a cabinet or a hutch than a television set. Not only was it light years behind in modern technology, but the knob to change the channels was broken. We got so desperate to change the channel that we ordered cable service just so we could have a remote control through the cable box!

After some great years together, there came a day (a sad day) that we had to part with *the legend*. It was the end of an era. Yes, we broke down and bought ourselves a new TV, with this "new fangled" 21st-century technology. And while we needed extensive training in order to operate this new machine, we did admire some of its features (including changing the channel). One of the greatest features was "PIP" or *picture-in-picture*. We can now simultaneously watch two channels. (I am sure the guy who designed this feature must have certainly been a sports fanatic!)

TWO REALMS

The world in which we live is similar to PIP technology. We live in a world that has two channels operating simultaneously on the one screen of our lives. For our purposes, we will call these screens "realms." One realm we are readily familiar with is the natural (or physical) realm. Our five natural senses are designed to help us navigate this realm. The second realm is the invisible (or spiritual) realm. Some refer to the latter realm as the *heavenlies* realm, as it is referred to in the book of Ephesians.

Your "world" is comprised of these two realms. The world as a planet is comprised of these two realms. Most people are ignorant of the truth surrounding this reality. Many followers of Christ live under the same ignorance. Living in this ignorance has serious consequences for all of us; while living in the truth reaps great rewards. Most people (including believers) unknowingly live under much difficulty, ruin, and hardship due to being ignorant about this truth. Most people from Western cultures are particularly unaware of how the spiritual realm affects our everyday lives.

The Bible provides us with a PIP feature in the first two chapters of Job (among many other Biblical accounts).

There is one world that Job lived in; yet the two realms of his world are simultaneously featured for our viewing. In this Biblical account, we can graphically see how the two realms interface. While we briefly look at this account, realize that Job lived in the same world we do: One with two realms.

JOB'S WORLD IS ROCKED – A LOOK AT THE NATURAL REALM

The first couple of chapters of Job give a simultaneous view of both realms. If you casually read Job 1:13-19 and 2:7-10, and were limited to seeing only the natural realm, you would assume that Job simply had a series of disastrous misfortunes.

Job 1:13-19 (NASB) *Now it happened on the day when his sons and his daughters were eating and drinking wine in their oldest brother's house, that a messenger came to Job and said, "The oxen were plowing and the donkeys feeding beside them, and the Sabeans attacked and took them. They also slew the servants with the edge of the sword, and I alone have escaped to tell you." While he was still speaking, another also came and said, "The fire of God fell from heaven and burned up the sheep and the servants and consumed them, and I alone have escaped to tell you." While he was still speaking, another also came and said, "The Chaldeans formed three bands and made a raid on the camels and took them and slew the servants with the edge of the sword; and I alone have escaped to tell you." While he was still speaking, another also came and said, "Your sons and your daughters were eating and drinking wine in their oldest brother's house, and behold, a great wind came from across the wilderness and struck the four corners of the house, and it fell on the young people and they died; and I alone have escaped to tell you."*

Job 2:7-10 (NASB) *. . . smote Job with sore boils from the sole of his foot to the crown of his head. And he took a potsherd to scrape himself while he was sitting among the ashes. Then his wife said to him, "Do you still hold fast your integrity? Curse God and die!" But he said to her, "You speak as one of the foolish women speaks. Shall we indeed accept good from God and not accept adversity?" In all this Job did not sin with his lips.*

Job's world became a tumultuous storm, and nothing in his life was left untouched. His livelihood was destroyed when he lost his herds, flocks, and servants to marauding thugs. Job's adult children lost their lives in a freak storm. He then became riddled with ill-health, and his relationship with his wife disintegrated. The bottom line is that he was in financial ruin, lost his entire family, and had to withstand the emotional abandonment of his wife. Our first response to such a situation in the Western culture might be to contact a law enforcement agency or security company, a financial advisor, subscribe to the weather channel, or locate a marriage counselor. Our mindset is always on the physical so we begin asking, "How can I get my life back on course?" We give no thought to what might be going on "behind the scenes."

A BEHIND THE SCENES LOOK AT THE HEAVENLIES REALM

If we look more closely at the Biblical account of Job, we realize there is another significant factor to the story. It is in regard to a realm not comprised of flesh and blood, nor that which is physical; it is the spiritual realm.

Job 1:6-12 (NASB) *Now there was a day when the sons of God came to present themselves before the Lord, and Satan also came among them. And the Lord said to Satan, "From where do you come?" Then Satan answered the Lord and said, "From roaming about on the earth and walking around on it." And the Lord said to Satan, "Have you considered My servant Job? For there is no one like him on the earth, a blameless and upright man, fearing God and turning away from evil." Then Satan answered the Lord, "Does Job fear God for nothing? Hast Thou not made a hedge about him and his house and all that he has, on every side? Thou hast blessed the work of his hands, and his possessions have increased in the land. But put forth Thy hand now and touch all that he has; he will surely curse Thee to Thy face." Then the Lord said to Satan, "Behold, all that he has is in your power, only do not put forth your hand on him." So Satan departed from the presence of the Lord.*

Job 2:1-7 (NASB) *Again there was a day when the sons of God came to present themselves before the Lord, and Satan also came among them to present himself before the Lord. And the Lord said to Satan, "Where have you come from?" Then Satan answered the Lord and said, "From roaming about on the earth, and walking around on it." And the Lord said to Satan, "Have you considered My servant Job? For there is no one like him on the earth, a blameless and upright man fearing God and turning away from evil. And he still holds fast his integrity, although you incited Me against him, to ruin him without cause." And Satan answered the Lord and said, "Skin for skin! Yes, all that a man has he will give for his life. However, put forth Thy hand, now, and touch his bone and his flesh; he will curse Thee to Thy face." So the Lord said to Satan, "Behold, he is in your*

power, only spare his life." Then Satan went out from the presence of the Lord, and smote Job with sore boils from the sole of his foot to the crown of his head.

From the above text, we readily see that Satan is very aware of people and events on earth—in fact, we read that Satan roams about and walks around on the earth. These verses also demonstrate that Satan is limited by mankind's actions of righteousness and God's sovereign love and protection. But, we also recognize in the above texts, that Satan can energize people to commit crimes against other people and property, he can manipulate the weather to accomplish his objectives, he can affect the physical health of people, and his kingdom can influence people's relationships with one another.

We clearly see Job's world comprised of two realms—the *natural realm* and the *spiritual realm*. The following diagram might help illustrate this point for us.

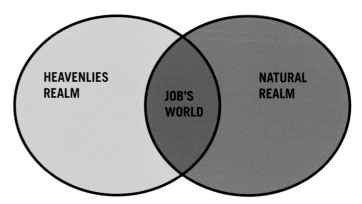

For the sake of illustration in making the two realms distinct, the circles are somewhat separated. But reality is that both realms completely overlap and interface to comprise our world. In fact, this diagram reflects all of life upon this earth. We live in one world with two realms—a spiritual and a physical realm, or the *heavenlies* and the *natural*. There is no person or institution that does not live in both realms.

THE HEAVENLIES REALM

The book of Ephesians speaks directly to the spiritual realm, the *heavenlies*. Our five natural senses are not readily attuned to this realm. Though invisible and spiritual, this realm is nevertheless real. Paul addresses this realm throughout the book of Ephesians, and he specifically speaks to it in the following verses.

Ephesians 1:3 (NASB) *Blessed be the God and Father of our Lord Jesus Christ, who has blessed us with every spiritual blessing in the **heavenly places** in Christ.*

Ephesians 1:20 (NASB) *which He brought about in Christ, when He raised Him from the dead and seated Him at His right hand in the **heavenly places**.*

Ephesians 2:6 (NASB) *and raised us up with Him, and seated us with Him in the* **heavenly places** *in Christ Jesus.*

Ephesians 3:10 (NASB) *so that the manifold wisdom of God might now be made known through the church to the rulers and the authorities in the heavenly places.*

Ephesians 6:12 (NASB) *For our struggle is not against flesh and blood, but against the rulers, against the powers, against the world forces of this darkness, against the spiritual forces of wickedness in the* **heavenly places**.

The English words "heavenly *places*" are taken from the Greek word *epouranios*. You will notice the word "places" is in italics. The word "places" is added by translators in an effort to give further explanation to the Greek word's meaning. There is no other Greek word that is translated "places." This effort of the translators is unfortunate in one sense because the word communicates more than a location or place. It would be better understood as a realm, or economy of existence. The word *epouranios* is used at least seventeen times in the New Testament to describe *things, bodies, glory, essence, callings, gifts, governments, economy of existence, as well as a city* (the heavenly city, Jerusalem). The word fundamentally describes the essence and economy of the spiritual realm. The word *epouranios* would be better translated simply by the word "heavenlies," or possibly by the words "heavenly realms."

To repeat for the purpose of clarification; the word *epouranios* does not communicate merely spatial location as much as a realm of existence, economy, and/or function. In other words, this realm is not "out there somewhere." It is present everywhere! All spiritual realities and bodies make up the heavenlies realm. This realm includes: God the Father who is Spirit, Jesus Christ (the Son), the Holy Spirit, angels, and Satan and his demonic powers of darkness. Other spiritual dynamics include the reality of blessings and curses, righteousness and sin, words and prayers. It is as real and distinct in its essence as the difference between how life functions under the ocean, versus life above the ocean. To live in the depths of the ocean requires a body that can exist and function in that environment. There are laws that govern life and existence in the ocean that are different from the laws that govern life above the water. Likewise, what sets the heavenlies realm apart from the natural realm is the economy of existence and function.

This realm exists within human beings. The Holy Spirit indwells believers (Romans 8:9), and angels press in close as they minister to us (Hebrews 1:13-14). We also know, through the Scriptures and ministry experience, that people can be demonized in varying degrees (Mark 5 and 2 Corinthians 12:7). Demons did not just influence and energize people in Biblical times; it is still a reality today. There is also activity in the *heavenlies realm* that is over territories of world empires and nations (we will get into this later in the text). There are wars that are going on right now out there in the heavens (distinct from the heavenlies; for the heavens are places of location while the heavenlies merely speaks to a realm).

THE NATURAL REALM

The second realm can be identified as the *realm of the natural.* This realm is *visible* and the five natural senses operate very well in this realm. We readily see, hear, feel, taste, and smell in this realm. This realm can also be identified as the *physical realm.* Historically, Western culture has been preoccupied with this realm (comprised of flesh and blood; the physical). Many other cultures are more attuned to the *spiritual realm* than are those of us from Western cultures, where empirical evidence—that which can be physically observed and tested repetitively to validate reality—is relied upon heavily. The solution for most problems or mysteries is first searched for in the natural or physical realm. It is not uncommon for people to believe, "If you can't touch it, see it, smell it, taste it, and hear it physically, it isn't real." In contrast (for better or for worse) many other cultures first look for a solution to problems or mysteries in the spiritual realm.

THE REALITY OF THE INVISIBLE

In talking with Nicodemus in John 3, Jesus used the analogy of the wind to describe the working of the Holy Spirit. He pointed out that one cannot see the wind or the source of the wind, but one sees the effects of the wind. A modern illustration Is wireless technology. Now, you already know that I am technologically challenged. So I am baffled by the ability to use my cell phone to contact someone on his or her cell phone in another part of the world. I understand that there are invisible signals from my cell phone that communicate with a satellite, and then that satellite communicates invisible signals to the receiving cell phone. With the natural physical eye, who sees the signals?! Yet despite the fact that we cannot see the signals, millions of people use cell phones every day!

The *heavenlies realm* is similar. We may not be able to physically perceive the components of the *heavenlies realm*, but that does not diminish its reality. Our lives are affected and influenced greatly by that which comprises the *heavenlies*. In fact, I would go so far as to say that what transpires in our physical world is the majority of the time the result of what has already transpired in the *heavenlies realm*. In turn, how we live our lives in the natural realm influences what happens in the *heavenlies*.

NOTES:

FREEDOM CLASS
Resource Section

[104]   The Christian Birthright Card
[106]   God's Love and Forgiveness
[108]   Walking in the Opposite Spirit

[1] THE CHRISTIAN'S BIRTHRIGHT

I am the light of the world, and the darkness cannot suppress it. **Matthew 5:14**

I am living in Christ's authority which gives me power over all of the power of the enemy. **Luke 10:17-20**

I am part of the true vine, a channel of Christ's life and energy. **John 15:1, 5**

I am not condemned, but declared fully forgiven and righteous in Christ. **Romans 8:1**

I am a joint-heir with Christ, sharing His inheritance with Him. **Romans 8:17**

I am secure in Christ's love for me. **Romans 8:35-39**

I am an overwhelming conqueror in Christ against all that would come against me. **Romans 8:37-39**

I am a temple—a dwelling place of God. His spirit and His life dwell in me. **1 Corinthians 3:16; 6:19**

I am united to the Lord and am one spirit with Him. **1 Corinthians 6:17**

I am a member of Christ's body. **1 Corinthians 12:27; Ephesians 5:30**

I am a new creation in Christ, old things are passing away. **2 Corinthians 5:17**

I am reconciled to God and am a minister of reconciliation for God to others. **2 Corinthians 5:18-19**

I am righteous with God's righteousness. **2 Corinthians 5:21**

I am a child of God and one in Christ. **Galatians 3:26, 28**

I am a child of God, my personal heavenly Father, who intimately and infinitely loves me. **Galatians 4:6**

I am an heir of God since I am a child of God. **Galatians 4:6-7**

I am a saint. **Ephesians 1:1; 1 Corinthians 1:2; Philippians 1:1; Colossians 1:2**

I am seated in the heavenly realm, with Christ, in all His authority over Satan's kingdom. **Ephesians 1:19-23; 2:5-6**

I am God's workmanship, his handiwork, born anew in Christ to do His work. **Ephesians 2:10**

I am a fellow citizen with the rest of God's family. **Ephesians 2:19**

I am the light of God and expose the darkness by Christ's life in me. **Ephesians 2:19**

I am a warrior against Satan and fully outfitted to stand triumphant in Christ. **Ephesians 6:10-20**

I am hidden with Christ in God, so Satan must go through Christ to get to me. **Colossians 3:3**

I am an expression of the life of Christ because He is my life. **Colossians 3:4**

I am chosen of God, holy and dearly loved, and therefore jealously protected. **Colossians 3:12;**
1 Thessalonians 1:4

I am a holy partaker of a heavenly calling. **Hebrews 3:1**

I am a partaker of Christ; I share in His life. **Hebrews 3:14**

I am one of God's living stones, being built up in Christ as a spiritual house. **1 Peter 2:5**

I am a member of a chosen race, a royal priesthood, a holy nation, a people of God's own choosing.
1 Peter 2:9-10

I am an alien and a stranger in this world in which I temporarily live. **1 Peter 2:11**

I am an enemy of the devil. **1 Peter 5:8**

I am a child of God and I will resemble Christ when He returns. **1 John 3:1-2**

I am born of God, and the evil one—the devil—must go through God to touch me. **1 John 5:18**

[2] GOD'S LOVE AND FORGIVENESS

1 Chronicles 16:34 (NASB)
O give thanks to the Lord, for He is good; for His love endures forever.

Psalm 32:10 (NIV)
Many are the woes of the wicked, but the LORD's unfailing love surrounds the man who trusts in him.

Psalm 57:10 (NIV)
For great is Your love, reaching to the heavens; Your faithfulness reaches to the skies.

Psalm 86:13 (NIV)
For great is Your love toward me; You have delivered me from the depths of the grave.

Psalm 103:17 (NIV)
But from everlasting to everlasting the LORD's love is with those who fear him, and his righteousness with their children's children.

Psalm 106:1 (NIV)
Praise the LORD. Give thanks to the LORD, for he is good; his love endures forever.

Psalm 107:1, 8, 43 (NIV)
Give thanks to the LORD, for he is good; his love endures forever. . . Let them give thanks to the LORD for his unfailing love and his wonderful deeds for men . . . Whoever is wise, let him heed these things and consider the great love of the LORD.

Psalm 117:1, 2 (NIV)
Praise the LORD, all you nations; extol him, all you peoples. For great is his love toward us, and the faithfulness of the LORD endures forever.

Psalm 145:8 (NIV)
The LORD is gracious and compassionate, slow to anger and rich in love.

Isaiah 38:17 (NIV)
Surely it was for my benefit that I suffered such anguish. In your love you kept me from the pit of destruction; you have put all my sins behind your back.

Jeremiah 31:3 (NIV)
The LORD appeared to us in the past, saying: I have loved you with an everlasting love; I have drawn you with loving-kindness.

Joel 2:13 (NIV)

*Rend your heart and not your garments. Return to the L*ORD *your God, for he is gracious and compassionate, slow to anger and abounding in love, and he relents from sending calamity.*

Zephaniah 3:17 (NASB)

The Lord your God is in your midst, a victorious warrior. He will exult over you with joy, He will be quiet in His love, He will rejoice over you with shouts of joy.

John 3:16 (NIV)

For God so loved the world that he gave his one and only Son, that whoever believes in him shall not perish but have eternal life.

Romans 8:38-39 (NIV)

For I am convinced that neither death nor life, neither angels, nor demons, neither the present nor the future, nor any powers, neither height nor depth, nor anything else in all creation, will be able to separate us from the love of God that is in Christ Jesus our Lord.

Ephesians 2:4-5 (NIV)

But because of His great love for us, God, who is rich in mercy, made us alive with Christ even when we were dead in transgressions—it is by grace you have been saved.

1 John 3:1 (NIV)

How great is the love the Father has lavished on us, that we should be called children of God! And that is what we are! The reason the world does not know us is that it did not know Him.

Nehemiah 9:17 (NIV)

They refused to listen and failed to remember the miracles you performed among them. They became stiff-necked and in their rebellion appointed a leader in order to return to their slavery. But you are a forgiving God, gracious and compassionate, slow to anger and abounding in love. Therefore, you did not desert them. . . .

Psalm 103:1-3 (NIV)

*Praise the L*ORD*, O my soul; all my inmost being, praise His holy name. Praise the L*ORD*, O my soul, and forget not all His benefits—who forgives all your sins and heals all your diseases. . .*

Psalm 103: 8, 10, 11, 14 (NIV)

*The L*ORD *is compassionate and gracious, slow to anger, abounding in love. He does not treat us as our sins deserve or repay us according to our iniquities. For as high as the heavens are above the earth, so great is His love for those who fear Him; . . . for He knows how we are formed, He remembers that we are dust.*

Lamentations 3:22 (NIV)

Because of the L*ORD*'s great love we are not consumed, for his compassions never fail.

[3] WALKING IN THE OPPOSITE SPIRIT

Instead of anger:
I do not let anger gain control over me; I think about it and remain silent. (Psalm 4:4)
I do not let the sun go down on my anger. (Ephesians 4:26)
I am prayerful and patient in the midst of trouble. (Romans 12:12)
I do not pay back evil for evil, but I am patient and do good to everyone. (1 Thessalonians 5:14)
I continue to show deep love for others as love covers a multitude of sins. (1 Peter 4:8)
It is Christ's love that controls me in whatever I do. (2 Corinthians 5:14)

Instead of control:
I trust the Lord with all my heart, not leaning on my own understanding. (Proverbs 3:5)
I do not control others but I think of them as better than myself. (Philippians 2:3)
I am gentle and show true humility to everyone. (Titus 3:2)
I clothe myself with compassion, kindness, humility and gentleness. (Colossians 3:12)
I live in a manner that respects and submits to others. (1 Peter 2:13-14)
I am the servant of others. (Luke 14:43)
I will never be in want for anything because I know the Lord is my shepherd. (Psalm 23:1)

Instead of competing with others:
I am a servant of Christ. (Matthew 23:11)
In humility I consider others better than myself. (Philippians 2:3)
I look out for the interests of others. (Philippians 2:4)
I am a servant of all. (Matthew 23:11)
I do good to all people. (Galatians 6:10)
I am an encourager of others and I love my brothers and sisters in Christ. (1 Thessalonians 5:14)

Instead of criticizing others:
I speak in a way that is helpful to others. (Job 16:4-5)
I cover all offences with love. (Proverbs 17:9)
I do not judge or condemn others but only forgive. (Matthew 7:1-2; Luke 6:37)
I bear the failings of those who are weak and purpose not to please myself. (Romans 15:1)
I carry the burdens of others without comparing myself to them. (Galatians 6:1)
I put on love and forgive all grievances I might have towards others. (Colossians 3:13-14)
I am merciful and speak and act without judgement. (James 2:12-13)
I do not speak against, slander, or judge my neighbour. (James 4:11-12)

Instead of being fearful:
I do not fear when the heat comes; my confidence is in the Lord. (Jeremiah 17:7-8)
I am kept safe because of my trust in the Lord and I will not fear man. (Proverbs 29:25)
I have been given a spirit of power, love and self discipline, not fear. (2 Timothy 1:7)
I have no fear of punishment because perfect love casts out fear. (1 John 4:18)
I have no fear in my heart because the Lord protects me from danger. (Psalm 27:1-3)
I am not afraid when I lie down because my sleep will be sweet. (Proverbs 3:24)
I am not afraid of bad news; my heart is steadfast, trusting in the Lord. (Psalm 112:7)

I am not afraid because you are close beside me. (Psalm 23:4)
I do not fear anything except the Lord. He will keep me safe. (Isaiah 8:13)
I am no longer a slave to the fear of dying, for He will deliver me. (Hebrews 2:14-15)

Instead of feeling hopeless:
I put my hope in your word, for you are my refuge and my shield. (Psalm 119:114)
I put my hope in your unfailing love, and I know your eyes are upon me. (Psalm 33:18)
I believe you delight in me because I put my hope in your unfailing love. (Psalm 147:11)
I know that because I hope in you, You will renew my strength; I will soar on wings like eagles; I will run
and not grow weary; I will walk and not faint. (Isaiah 40:31)
I hope in the Lord, and He does not disappoint me. (Isaiah 49:23)
I will not be disappointed because God pours out His love into my heart. (Romans 5:5)
I know that God gives me hope and will keep me happy and full of peace. (Romans 15:13)
I will overflow with hope through the power of the Holy Spirit. (Romans 15:13)
Since I have such hope, I am very bold. (2 Corinthians 3:12)

Instead of inferiority:
I will not covet what others have. (Exodus 20:17)
I am chosen by God to do the good works that He has prepared for me to do! (Ephesians 2:10)
I am strong and I do not fear, for my God will come. (Isaiah 35:4)
I am the salt of the earth and the light of the world. (Matthew 5:13-14)
I am a spirit-powered witness of Christ. (Acts 1:8)
I am God's workmanship. (Ephesians 2:10)
I am highly favoured by God, and He is with me. (Luke 1:28)
I am a mighty warrior, and the Lord is with me. (Judges 6:12)
I am confident of God's unconditional love for me. (1 John 3:1)
I have been given a spirit of power, love and self-discipline and not fear. (2 Timothy 1:7)

Instead of insecurity:
I am secure because nothing will separate me from the love of Christ. (Romans 8:38)
I am complete in Christ. (Colossians 2:10)
I have been chosen and appointed by God to bear fruit. (John 15:16)
I may approach God with freedom and confidence. (Ephesians 3:12)
The kingdom of God is within me. (Luke 17: 20-21)
He directs my path when I seek Him. (Proverbs 3:5-6)
I am fearfully and wonderfully made. (Psalm 139:10)
I am free from condemnation. (Romans 8:1-2)
I am God's workmanship, created for good works. (Ephesians 2:10)
I cannot be separated from the love of God. (Romans 8:35-39)

Instead of jealousy and envy:
I am complete in Christ. (Colossians 2:10)
I am assured that all things work together for good. (Romans 8:28)
I have been chosen and appointed by God to bear fruit. (John 15:16)
I am a temple of God. (1 Corinthians 3:16)
I am God's workmanship, created for good works. (Ephesians 2:6)
The Lord is my shepherd; I shall not want. You anoint my head with oil, my cup overflows. Surely goodness
and love will follow me all the days of my life. (Psalms 23:1, 5-6)
I am satisfied—I am fulfilled—I am full of joy and I am free.

Instead of being passive:

I walk after the Lord my God and fear Him, and I keep His commandments and obey His voice. I shall serve Him and hold fast to Him. (Deuteronomy 13:4)

I am diligent to the very end and am not lazy. (Proverbs 10:4)

I work hard and show my love for God by loving and caring for others. (Hebrews 6:10-11)

I have been chosen and appointed to bear fruit. (John 15:16)

I am God's co-worker. (2 Corinthians 6:1)

I can do all things through Him who strengthens me. (Philippians 4:13)

I have not been given a spirit of timidity, but of power, love and sound mind. (2 Timothy 1:7)

I am not lazy, but I imitate those who through faith and patience inherit what has been promised. (Hebrews 6:11-12)

Instead of pride and arrogance:

I hate pride and arrogance, evil behaviour, and perverse speech. (Proverbs 8:13)

I am wise to take advice from others because pride only breeds quarrels. (Proverbs 13:10)

I choose to walk in humility and let God do the exalting. (Luke 4:11)

I am the servant of others. (Luke 14:43)

I do not boast about myself, but my approval comes from the Lord. (2 Corinthians 10:10)

I love others. I do not boast; I am not proud or self-seeking. (2 Corinthians 13:4-5)

I have humbled myself under God's mighty hand, and He will raise me up. (1 Peter 5:6)

I am not selfish but think of others as better than myself. (Philippians 2:3)

I do not live to make a good impression on others. (Philippians 2:3)

I do not look to my own interests but only to the interests of others. (Philippians 2:4)

I clothe myself with compassion, kindness, humility, and gentleness. (Colossians 3:12)

I am gentle and show true humility to everyone. (Titus 3:2)

Instead of rebellion:

I am obedient to God's truth and therefore am loved by Him. (John 14:21)

I purpose to do nothing without consulting the Father. (John 5:30)

I seek His will and not my own will on everything. (Matthew 26:39)

I live in submission to those God has placed in authority. (Romans 13:1-2)

I understand that those in authority have been placed there by God. (Hebrews 13:7)

I live in a manner that respects and submits to others. (1 Peter 2:13-14)

I honor all people and seek to support and protect their honor. (1 Peter 2:17)

Instead of rejection:

I am confident of God's unconditional love for me. (I John 3:1)

I forgive and bless all those who have hurt or rejected me. (Matthew 6:12; Ephesians 3:31-32)

I am loving and confident even when I fear people will reject me. (I John 4:18)

I am secure because nothing will separate me from the love of Christ. (Romans 8:38)

I rejoice because the Lord has rescued me and has been so good to me. (Psalms 13:1,5-6)

I am not forsaken by the Lord for He is the stronghold of my life. (Psalms 27:1,10)

I have been chosen by God and am not rejected. (Isaiah 41:9)

I do not fear for He is with me to strengthen, help me and uphold me. (Isaiah 41:10)

I know that the Lord takes great delight in me and rejoices over me. (Zephaniah 3:17)